Stuart Morris was born on Portland in 1942. His interest in local history was fostered by the discovery of his family's involvement with quarrying, Portland Breakwater, fishing and even smuggling. A Dorset County Councillor for 12 years, he is a long-term campaigner for the local environment and has served as Portland Town Mayor. A civil engineer by profession, he retired as Highways Agency Manager for the local Borough Council in 2000. Stuart's interests include technology, photography, videography, world affairs, music and the arts. He has made several radio and TV appearances. He is married to Heather, with children and grandchildren. His previous books include: *Portland: An Illustrated History, Portland Camera, 'Discover Dorset' Portland, Portland, A Portrait in Colour, Weymouth, A Portrait in Colour,* and *Portland Then and Now.*

IN THE SAME SERIES

DORSET: The Army
George Forty

DORSET: The Royal Air Force
Colin Pomeroy

Following page
Exuding the power of the great battleships, but nearing the end of her career, the 22 year-old HMS *Nelson* leaves Portland Harbour in 1947.

DORSET
THE ROYAL NAVY

STUART MORRIS

THE DOVECOTE PRESS

A Lynx helicopter of RNAS Portland flies over HMS *Minerva*,
powering through a heavy sea off Dorset in 1987.
An award-winning photograph by Chris North of HMS *Osprey*
(Crown Copyright).

First published in 2011 by The Dovecote Press Ltd
Stanbridge, Wimborne Minster, Dorset BH21 4JD

ISBN 978-1-904-34988-4

© Stuart Morris 2011
Stuart Morris has asserted his rights under the Copyright, Designs
and Patent Act 1988 to be identified as author of this work

Typeset in FSIngrid and designed by The Dovecote Press Ltd
Printed and bound by GraphyCems, Navarra

All papers used by The Dovecote Press are natural, recyclable products
made from wood grown in sustainable, well-managed forests

A CIP catalogue record for this book is available from the British Library

1 3 5 7 9 8 6 4 2

CONTENTS

ONE

ORIGINS

For some 200 years the British Navy was the most powerful in the world. It was instrumental in establishing the British Empire as the dominant world power from the beginning of the nineteenth century until the Second World War. Its origins go back many hundreds of years, and in the twenty-first century the historically smaller Royal Navy continues to play a crucial role on the international stage.

Throughout its history Dorset was a tranquil, pastoral county with no great towns or industries to attract particular attention from would-be aggressors. However the security of the adjoining English Channel has always been vital to the nation and Dorset's coastline was vulnerable. It was a soft place to attack, with many undefended landing places. The Romans invaded these shores, and in 789 the Vikings made their first attack on the British mainland at Portland.

It was in response to those raids that England's first Navy of sorts was established in the ninth century by Alfred the Great, but it was not sustained. King John resurrected a Navy during the twelfth and thirteenth centuries with a fleet of 500 ships. The Navy went into successful action against the French off Dorset and along the Channel during the Hundred Years War, but the force again declined.

France and Spain were the traditional enemies of Great Britain for centuries, and rivalry and posturing by respective leaders compounded the friction which arose all too frequently.

Portland Castle was completed in about 1540, one of a string of coastal forts. Henry VIII's naval fleet of nearly 60 ships was already a force to be reckoned with, but these coastal bulwarks were vital backstops against feared French and Spanish attacks.

6

A detail from the bird's-eye view of the Dorset coast drawn in the wake of a survey by Sir John Russell in 1539 for Henry VIII, with Melcombe Regis (Weymouth) in the bottom centre. Although war with France then seemed imminent, the forts and beacons illustrated were only recommendations and not all were built. Sandsfoot and Portland castles are clearly shown, and were positioned to provide crossfire over the anchorage at Portland Roads.

The first properly constituted 'Navy Royal', as it was then called, was in the reign of Henry VIII in the sixteenth century when the traditional rivalry between England and France led to the brink of war.

In 1538 the fear of invasion peaked, and Henry ordered a chain of new fortifications to be built along the south coast, including Portland Castle (1539) and Sandsfoot Castle (1541) to protect the Portland Roads, which was well established as an important haven for all types of shipping.

By the time of Henry's death in 1547, the country had a powerful naval fleet of 58 vessels which regularly sailed past the Dorset coast, and took advantage of its natural havens.

The county's most useful anchorages were in Poole Harbour and the naturally sheltered lee side of Portland and Weymouth. However, in 1586 Dorset's Deputy Lieutenants reported to the Privy Council that Portland and Sandsfoot castles were incapable of protecting these expansive waters, and 'the enemy's fleet could ride there altogether out of range'. The great strategist Walter Raleigh knew the importance of Portland Roads, and in 1587 he urged Queen Elizabeth's chief advisor Lord Burghley to strengthen its defences.

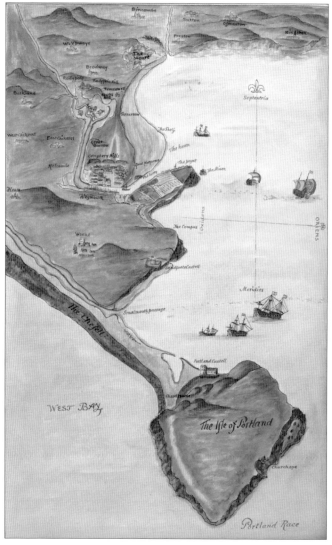

From the earliest days, ships of the Royal Navy needed the valuable anchorages of Portland Roads and Weymouth Bay. Chesil Beach and the high bulk of the Island of Portland gave natural shelter from prevailing south-westerly winds.

Throughout Elizabeth's reign the naval ships were augmented by armed merchantmen, provided – under protest – by coastal towns such as Lyme, Weymouth, and Poole. The civilian ships inspired confidence by their numbers but the brunt of fighting was always borne by the men-of-war.

Spain had now become the leading naval power in Europe. The Spanish both feared and despised anti-Catholic England and its Protestant queen. In 1588 they dispatched their great Armada to destroy the English fleet, and ultimately to depose Elizabeth.

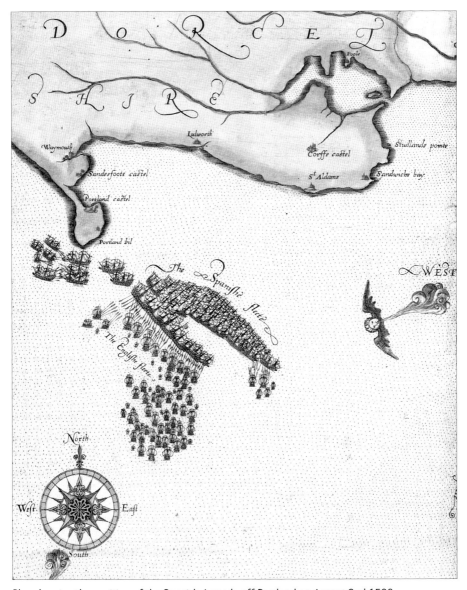

Plan showing the position of the Spanish Armada off Portland on August 2nd 1588.

The Armada was first sighted off the Scilly Isles by Captain Fleming on the bark *Golden Hind* on 29 July 1588. Beacons were lit along the coast, and military forces assembled at Weymouth, where a landing was expected. But the unpredictable Armada was intent on sailing on up the Channel, in a huge crescent formation.

This was a time of profound change in sea warfare. The outmoded Spanish galleons were cumbersome, riding high out of the water with towering fore and after castles from which handheld firearms could be discharged. Their height and broad beam made these ships awkward to sail. The English ships were of a new

9

advanced design; smaller, faster and much more manoeuvrable.

Dorset was now to witness one of the great engagements between the Spanish and the English.

Lord Howard chased the Armada up the Channel, catching up with them off Portland Bill on 2 August 1588. In a fresh wind the ships tried to out-manoeuvre each other, and the boom of their gunfire carried easily to Weymouth: 'Never was heard greater thundering of ordnance on both sides,' wrote Camden. Martin Frobisher in the *Triumph* knew of the perils posed by the Shambles Bank and the tidal race off the Bill, the Spaniards did not. The English outwitted the enemy at every move, blasting broadsides each time wind and current brought them into range. Lord Howard ordered six ships to follow him in a line-ahead attack, but they failed to get close enough to inflict terminal damage.

By the end of the day-long Battle of Portland the English had run out of ammunition, but the Spanish, although not yet crushed, had been decisively routed.

The Spanish Armada, of course, was eventually defeated by the English and Dutch fleets, and by the weather. Within 10 years Philip of Spain was dying and Spain was in no state to wage any further attacks.

The English Civil War prompted a rapid expansion of England's Navy from the 1650s, organised by the distinguished Admiral or 'General-at-Sea' Robert Blake. Despite having little maritime experience, Blake was a firm leader; he had made his name during a series of sieges for Parliament during the Civil War, including taking command of Lyme Regis in 1644.

By 1652 tensions were rising between England and the newly formed Dutch Republic, mainly over territorial control along the English Channel. The Dutch Navy was keen to be in command of the vital trading routes, but they met their match in February 1653. The English fleet had been refitted and reorganised and 65 ships put to sea under Admirals Blake, Deane and Monck. Off Portland they sighted Van Tromp's 80-strong Dutch fleet, protecting a convoy of 200 merchantmen.

Admiral Penn in the *Speaker* was ahead of Blake in the *Triumph*. Confident with his much larger fleet Tromp made a sudden surprise attack. Blake turned to face the Dutch, and Penn's squadron followed. The *Triumph* found itself at the centre of a ferocious battle, and Blake was badly wounded in the thigh, while his flag captain and secretary were killed. When Monck's squadron joined with a brazen attack, the English gained immediate advantage. Some frigates veered from the main action to attack the Dutch escorts, causing Tromp to disengage from the mêlée to protect the convoy.

The first day of this 1653 Battle of Portland ended with a clear English victory. One English ship, the *Samson*, was sunk, and three more were forced back to port for repairs. At least three Dutch ships were sunk and another was burnt. The 40 guns *Struisvogel* was captured, albeit in a sorry state with masts shot away, and her decks running with the blood of the wounded and more than 80 dead crew.

Control of trading routes in the English Channel was the focus of a series of disputes between England and the Dutch Republic in the mid seventeenth century. This occasionally boiled over into a full engagement between the two navies, as here at the Battle of Portland in 1653.

On the next day, 28 February, the English again fired on the Dutch as they moved up the Channel. Tromp now deployed his warships in a defensive crescent formation to protect the merchantmen. In a fierce battle, the Dutch warships acted as a rearguard and successfully held off English attempts to break through the formation.

By nightfall the Dutch were running dangerously short of ammunition. In the darkness Tromp managed to manoeuvre around the English fleet, so by dawn he was away to the east, between the convoy and the English. The English gave chase and fighting resumed. Once again the Dutch came off worst, losing more vessels, and the convoy began to break up.

In this 3-day battle off Dorset the Dutch suffered 5 sunken warships; 2 burnt and 4 captured. Up to 50 of the 200 merchant ships in the convoy were taken. The English Navy was victorious.

Admiral Sir William Penn, who commanded the *Speaker* in the Battle of Portland, became MP for Weymouth in 1660. His son William became the founder of Pennsylvania USA and his wealthy great-grandson, John Penn, built the luxurious Pennsylvania Castle (1800) on a Portland clifftop, overlooking the site of his ancestor's sea battle.

In contrast to its 1653 victory, the English Navy suffered a crushing defeat in the second Anglo Dutch War (1665 to 1667). Stung by this and other defeats, efforts were redoubled to make the Royal Navy the strongest in the world.

TWO

TO COMMAND THE SEA

In the early eighteenth century the British Navy had more ships than any other nation, but several other countries were also expanding their fleets. The Royal Navy became preoccupied with enforcing British interests across the globe, and there was little activity directly affecting Dorset. However, France under Napoleon was becoming increasingly belligerent, and declared war on Britain in 1793.

The English Navy was desperately short of men, and in response a new defence force, the Sea Fencibles was created. This comprised boatmen and fishermen as well as part-time seafarers who were not liable to Impressment. The men were volunteers and were paid one shilling a day while on service. The Fencibles, however, failed to make an impression: Admiral St. Vincent was of the opinion that the Sea Fencibles were 'of no other use than to calm the fears of old ladies both within and without Parliament'.

Napoleon Bonaparte sought to invade Egypt as the first step in a campaign against British India. The result was the Battle of the Nile of 1798, now considered the most decisive naval engagement of the great age of sail. News of Rear-Admiral Lord Nelson's historic victory off Egypt reached King George III during one of his many summers in Weymouth with his family. This called for Royal celebrations, so on 8 October the decks of *St Florenzo* in Portland Roads were cleared for a grand celebratory dance. All the naval ships in the anchorage were dressed overall.

On one holiday at Weymouth the King's spirited young granddaughter, Princess Charlotte asked to go aboard HMS *Leviathan* lying in the bay. The connection from the shore was so choppy that two ladies and a bishop were soaked, greatly amusing the princess. Going aboard the *Leviathan* Charlotte insisted in climbing the ladder instead of being hoisted in the 'chair of state'. This caused much consternation as she had to remove her dress to do so!

On another occasion the warships *Magnificent* and *Southampton* were present in Weymouth Bay for royal protection. They showed off their skills by approaching each other at full sail at a fast closing speed, almost brushing gunports as they passed each other. HMS *Magnificent* had served in the American War of Independence and in the Napoleonic Wars. Both were eventually shipwrecked.

Hostilities with the French lasted for nine years; fighting lulled in 1802 but flared up again with a vengeance – in the Napoleonic Wars. The British Empire with its Royal Navy was soon to become the world's greatest power. There was no naval base between the ports of Portsmouth and Plymouth, but at times up to 140

George III's many visits to Weymouth (1789 to 1805) are normally associated with pleasure. However, whilst in Weymouth the King was never far from the flagships of his naval fleet, exercising in Weymouth Bay. He celebrated the historic victory in the Battle of the Nile in lavish style aboard the *St Fiorenzo* in Portland Roads. Latterly the royal party arrived on the magnificent yacht *Royal Sovereign*.

vessels could be seen assembled in the vast area of water sheltered, in most winds, by the huge bulk of Portland peninsula, the Chesil Bank and Weymouth.

In 1798 the Weymouth Corporation petitioned for a guard ship to lie in Portland Roads, but the Admiralty did not think that was justified. Portsmouth and Plymouth were considered the most likely places for attacks, and then only when the fleets were absent.

It was not the French who caused one of the Navy's worst disasters of the eighteenth century; it was nature. On 16th November 1795, Rear Admiral Christian set off from St Helens bound for the West Indies with a squadron of men-of-war and more than 200 military transports. The sight of that huge number of tall ships sailing away was described as 'truly magnificent'. The ships had 16,000 troops on board, as well as some women – wives of officers. Having rounded Portland Bill on the 17th they were caught in a terrible storm in West Bay. Some vessels made it to Torbay but others were blown back by storm force south-south-westerly winds. A dense fog descended, mingling the gale-whipped sea with the sky. 'They could distinguish nothing through the impenetrable gloom; hear nothing but the roaring of the wind. On the next day six transports went to pieces on Chesil Beach. Initially 234 bodies were washed ashore, but within days the beach was 'strewn for 2 miles with the dead bodies of men and animals, with pieces of wreck and piles plundered goods, which groups of people were at work to carry away.' By then more than 1600 had perished.

Undaunted, within just 22 days Rear Admiral Christian had recomposed his fleet and sailed again for the West Indies.

With the Napoleonic Wars under way, the Royal Navy found itself desperately short of men. Impressment was stepped up and the government required counties to conscript a specified number of men for the Navy, with an incentive of locally funded bounties. It was a perpetual struggle to raise enough men even by compulsion. In December 1652 the Mayor of Poole ordered a drum to be beaten through the town streets, to jolt men into 'volunteering' for the Navy. Seven years later Captain Fortesque of HMS *Prince Edward* took so many men off a Poole ship bound for Newfoundland that it was left undermanned, and it sank.

A notorious Press Gang event occurred at Portland in April 1803. In what became known as the Easton Massacre, Captain Wolfe of the frigate HMS *Aigle* had been ordered to get his quota from the Island. His naval gang of 29 men went ashore armed with muskets, bayonets, pistols and cutlasses and proceeded up over the Island, seizing likely young men as they went. The news had travelled ahead of them and by the time they reached Easton Square, quarrymen and fishermen were ready to resist. Who fired the first shots remains disputed, but in the struggle three men were shot dead, another was injured and a girl died later of her wounds. What the Portlanders knew and Wolfe probably did not, was that Royal Charters of 1453 and 1575 had freed Portlanders for ever from Admiralty jurisdiction, and the Navy therefore had no right to impress men on the Island.

The coroner's verdict was 'wilful murder' and Captain Wolfe, three officers and ten marines were charged. At Dorchester Assize they pleaded self defence, and to Portland's dismay were found not guilty of murder. Wolfe had claimed that the Islanders had fired first, but none were charged: a new war with France was looming and the Admiralty was keen to avoid any wider public resistance.

The first warship built in Dorset specifically for the Admiralty was a sloop of 270 tons built at Poole in 1746, but it was many years before others followed. Several men-of-war were built at Bridport from 1804, and others were built at Lyme, Portland, Weymouth, Swanage and Poole, although the latter was predominately building ships for its lucrative Newfoundland trade. From the reign of Henry VIII Bridport had the monopoly of supplying the Royal Navy with cordage, sailcloth, and nets; an industry which continued into the twentieth century.

THREE

ADMIRALS OF DORSET

Dorset has a long and proud seafaring tradition. Although not populous, many of her sons have played a sturdy part in England's maritime history. Countless men and officers who served and died for their country are now forgotten; others rose to high rank and national fame.

An early naval hero was Admiral Sir George Somers, who was born in Lyme Regis in 1554. He was involved in action against the Spanish Navy in 1595, and commanded several English ships between 1600 and 1602, including *Vanguard*, *Swiftsure* and *Warspite*. Somers's place in history was secured when he founded the English colony of Bermuda. He was knighted in 1603 and became MP for Lyme Regis in the same year.

The famous Hood dynasty had strong connections with Dorset. The Rev Samuel Hood, vicar of Thorncombe, was the father of two outstanding naval sons; Samuel and Alexander.

Samuel joined the Navy in 1740 and progressed right up to Admiral. In 1780, Admiral Hood sailed in command of a squadron to America at the time of their War of Independence. He became a Lord of the Admiralty in 1788 a post he held until the French war in 1793, retiring two years later aged 71.

Samuel's younger brother, Alexander, served in the Mediterranean and in the English Channel. He had great success while in command of the *Minerva*, including the retaking of the *Warwick*, a ship which the French had captured previously, after a six-hour fight in the Bay of Biscay. As a Rear Admiral of the Blue in 1782 he took command of the *Queen* (90 guns) serving in the Mediterranean. Later when Commander-in-Chief of the Channel fleet, and in reward for his sterling successes, he became Admiral Alexander Hood, Lord Bridport.

Henry Digby was just 13 when he joined the Navy. By his 30th birthday he had commanded several vessels, including HMS *Alcmene*. This was a lucrative period for him for he

Samuel Hood, later 1st Viscount Hood. Hood became friendly wih the young Nelson when both were serving in the Caribbean, and played an important role in furthering Nelson's career.

Above left Sir Henry Digby's career from a 13-year-old ship's boy to Admiral of the Blue was marked by incredible bravery, initiative – and good fortune. 'Prizes' from captured foreign ships had given him immense wealth, but his fame came with his bold actions commanding HMS *Africa* in the Battle of Trafalgar in 1805, when he was still only 34. Like Bullen and Hardy, Digby is wearing his Trafalgar medal.

Above right The son of naval surgeon John Bullen of Weymouth, Charles Bullen spent his formative childhood in Dorset. On the declaration of war with France in 1779, 11-year-old Charles joined the 64-gun *Europe*, the admiral's flagship. He could not have had a more adventurous and exciting career on both sides of the Atlantic, through numerous skirmishes, battles and even shipwrecks. In a single month in 1803 he captured 23 French merchantmen, and two years later was flag-captain in the 100-gun *Britannia* at Trafalgar.

succeeded in capturing numerous merchant ships, a French privateer, and a Spanish treasure ship which alone landed him prize money of over £40,000, a fortune at the time. Digby also played a crucial role in reducing smuggling in the English Channel

Hostilities with France escalated and in 1803 Henry Digby was given command of the small and aging HMS *Africa*. Two years later this third rate 64-gun ship of the line was thrust into the heart of the Battle of Trafalgar. Having found himself isolated from the main fleet, Digby ignored Admiral Nelson's signal to join the rest of the fleet, and brazenly sailed the *Africa* straight down the line of enemy ships, each of which carried more guns, firing broadsides as he went, until he eventually joined *Victory* in the mêlée.

A ferocious fight with the *Intrépide* ensued, and despite *Africa* losing 62 men killed or wounded – including most of her officers – the enemy ship surrendered.

Digby rose to Rear-Admiral in 1819, and became Admiral of the Blue in 1841. Having been knighted he retired to his magnificent manor at Minterne Magna, to enjoy the immense wealth from his prize money. The admiral's memorial in St Andrew's Church there sums up his career:

In Memory of
Henry Digby, K.C.B.,
Admiral of the 'Blue'
Born January 20, 1770; Died August 19, 1842
He Commanded H.M.S. 'Africa' in the memorable action off
Trafalgar, October 21, 1805. By his Gallantry and Daring
Obtained the marked approbation of Admiral Horatio,
Viscount Nelson, and the thanks of Parliament.

Richard Grindall (1750-1820), who married a Weymouth girl, joined the Navy at a very early age. After several victorious clashes with French ships, he was wounded in an action off Isle Croix, France. Grindall was Captain of HMS *Prince* at the Battle of Trafalgar. The 17-year-old *Prince* had the reputation of 'sailing like a haystack', so Nelson allowed her to make her own way into battle. She attacked the French *Achille*, which caught fire and exploded. Towards the end of the battle he took the surrender of the largest ship of the Spanish fleet, the *Santissima Trinidada*.

Vice-Admiral Grindall's son, Festing Horatio Grindall, a Weymouth lad, was a midshipman on board *Victory* at Trafalgar. His nephews, also from Dorset, served under him on board *Prince*. They were among some 180 Dorset men who served at the Battle of Trafalgar.

The famous sea battle of 21 October 1805 was fought off the south-west coast of Spain, just west of Cape Trafalgar. Twenty-seven British ships of the line led by Admiral Lord Nelson aboard HMS *Victory* roundly defeated the French and Spanish fleets. The Franco-Spanish force lost twenty-two ships, without a single British vessel being lost.

Commanding the 100-gun *Victory* was Nelson's long-time friend Thomas Masterman Hardy. Hardy was born in Kingston Russell in 1769. He went to Crewkerne Grammar School in Somerset, but left to join the Navy at just 12 years of age. Hardy worked his way through the naval ranks until he was serving as Lieutenant on the frigate HMS *Minerve* in 1796. That year, the ship came under the command of the then Captain Nelson. The *Minerve* was involved in several dangerous escapades in which Hardy proved his great tactical skills and seamanship. He was once captured by the Spanish, and only released in a prisoner exchange deal.

Hardy showed great humanity throughout his career. Once when the *Minerve* was being chased through the Straits of Gibraltar by the Spaniards, a crew member fell overboard. Hardy leaped into a jolly boat and rowed out to rescue him. However, the current separated the two boats and the Spanish were about to seize him again when Nelson turned his ship and came to his rescue.

Hardy was in the thick of action in the Battle of the Nile, and soon after was appointed the Flag Captain on HMS *Vanguard*. Thereafter he was Nelson's right-hand man in various conflicts, culminating in the Battle of Trafalgar in 1805.

Dorset-born Thomas Masterman Hardy is one of the most celebrated admirals in British naval history. Only 12 when he joined the Navy, he became Nelson's flag captain and was in command of HMS *Victory* at the Battle of Trafalgar. Hardy reached the apex of the naval service, becoming First Naval Lord at the Admiralty in 1830 and living long enough to witness the change from sail to steam.

Hardy, Nelson and King George III were all in Dorset when they first learned of the massing of Napoleon's fleet. On 15th September 1805 Hardy set sail on HMS *Victory* from Portsmouth with Nelson on board, and a month later the fleet confronted Napoleon's Navy near Cadiz. After the great battle which needs no retelling here, the *Victory* then struggled home against a strong gale, so it was a week before Hardy could write to his brother-in-law J.C. Manfield of Dorchester, to relate the tragic news of Nelson's death.

Problems of having wives and families aboard a naval ship were highlighted in this letter which Hardy wrote to his brother-in-law from the *Amphion*, while anchored in Portland Roads in 1802:

'*October 25th. 9 o-clock at night.*

'*We arrived here about two hours ago as Lady Robert Fitzgerald really could not stand the fatigues of the sea any longer, and how she is to get to Lisbon God only knows, as we have literally had fine with it ever since we left Spithead, which was only yesterday. The wind is not fair but we could make a very good start if I could prevail on them to allow me to proceed. If ever a married man was Blessed, the poor Lord Robert was last evening; and this morning out of the wife, eight children, as many female servants, secretary and six men servants, his Lordship had not a soul to put the children to bed and dressed in this morning, but the two women belonging to the ship.*'

A later note hints at the task of getting fresh supplies to the ship:

'*I have written this in hopes some Portland boat will call alongside of us in the Morning, or should the wind remain westerly I shall send a boat to Weymouth for fresh beef, but the moment the wind comes from the eastward – we shall be off.*'

Conditions for sailors at the time were appalling; dirt and misery, uneatable food,

Admiral Hardy lived in this fine Portesham house until his marriage to Louisa Berkeley in 1807.

verminous living conditions, weekly floggings, operations without anaesthetics on the dining table; enough to turn any sailor's stomach.

Sir Thomas Masterman Hardy went on to become First Lord of the Admiralty in November 1830, and was appointed Vice-Admiral of the Blue in 1837. He died in 1839. His Portesham manor house still looks much as it did when he lived there until his marriage in 1807.

To commemorate his achievements an octagonal tower 22m high, known as Hardy's Monument, was erected on Blackdown Hill above Portesham in 1844. The site had previously been selected by Hardy himself for the 'erection of a tall rick of furze faggots'; a beacon visible to distant ships going down the Channel. The tower was designed by Arthur Acland-Troyte and built by Henry Goddard of Bridport. Inside a spiral staircase leads to a high parapet giving a stunning panoramic view of southern Dorset. It was no folly; as intended, from the sea it became an invaluable landmark.

Early mariners depended on landmarks such as church towers and natural heights to navigate the poorly charted waters. Prominent points along on the Dorset coast were St Albans Chapel near Worth Matravers, the twin windmill towers on Portland and St Catherine's Chapel at Abbotsbury. Wyke Regis Church in conjunction with the north-east end of Portland was a leading mark to clear the Shambles.

Hilltop beacons were anciently lit to announce the approach of any feared enemy. Locations included Thorncombe, Beacon Hill, Poole, Norchard, Lewsdon, Cerne Abbas, Badbury, Bubb Down, Bulbarrow, Frampton, Lytchett, Ridegway, Verne and Branscombe hills on Portland, Woodbury, Penbury and Blackdown.

FOUR
A VULNERABLE COAST

Although the Battle of Trafalgar well and truly settled Britain's position in the world order, the government continued to agitate for a more effective Navy and better defended coasts. Portsmouth was the prime base for the Royal Navy, and Plymouth with its new breakwater was becoming established, but there were 135 miles between them. Of the existing harbours in mid-way Dorset, Poole was by nature impracticable because of the narrowness of its deepwater channels and Weymouth was too small to be of use for large numbers of mercantile or naval vessels. However Portland Roadstead offered tremendous prospects, if only it could be protected from south-easterly gales.

The most dynamic period in Dorset's association with the Royal Navy was without question the 150 years between the formation of Portland Harbour and the formal departure of the Royal Navy from the area just before the close of the twentieth century. The scheme to create a harbour from Portland Roads, and the subsequent establishment naval base, was of such a scale that it must dominate the rest of this narrative. The development had a major social and economic impact throughout the county.

The first serious proposal to form a harbour of the Roadstead was made by John Harvey, a successful Weymouth civil engineer, who published a booklet outlining his plans in 1794. There were often up to 150 merchantmen taking refuge from prevailing winds in the Roads. Harvey proposed a 2 mile long harbour wall of stone using some of the estimated 20 million tons of surplus rock lying behind the Island's East Cliffs. To convey the stone 'railways may be constructed with planes of such inclination as to carry them to the waterside without the aid of horses or engines'. The well-conceived idea was vigorously supported locally, but the government was yet to show any interest.

In 1825 the Lords Commissioners of the Admiralty announced their determination to proceed with the scheme, 'so as to form a commodious and safe harbour in the Roads, for his Majesty's men-of-war to ride at anchor, and to be enabled to put to sea when it would be quite impossible to do so from Spithead, thus in the case of any future war affording a complete check on the movement of an enemy Squadron from Cherbourg.'

In a pamphlet of 1827 John Harvey reaffirmed his ideas in some detail, pointing out that in rough weather the proposed harbour's central situation in the Channel would 'afford more advantages to the kingdom at large, than any similar

A momentous occasion in Dorset's maritime history: On 25 July 1849 HRH Prince Albert deposited the ceremonial stone to mark the start of the formation of the Portland Breakwaters. They were designed to enclose a strategic harbour of refuge, and as a foil to the great French harbour at Cherbourg, This was one of Victorian Britain's most ambitious, innovative and expensive civil engineering projects. This 1863 picture shows the Great Coaling Shed, centre right, one of the first facilities to be built. On the extreme right, smoke rises from the enormous creosote pressure chamber for impregnating the timber piles.

undertaking, there being no other port in which ships can ride with perfect safety between Portsmouth and Plymouth: it will afford a secure asylum to the merchant service in time of war, as well as form a most complete and efficient naval station, especially to watch the movements of the enemy: Fleets of every description could then at all times and seasons, and during all winds, rest perfectly secure'.

Captain Joseph Bennett had 12 years experience in command of the HM packet *Rover* between Weymouth and the Channel Islands. He had endured numerous gales while passing Portland, and had landed the mails at Weymouth during the 1795 storm which wrecked Admiral Christian's fleet in West Bay. He had often sheltered in Portland Roads in gales, and in making his case for a fortified harbour at Portland gave a graphic account of once anchoring there with 24 other vessels. 'We drove with both anchors ahead, and the whole of both cables cut to their extreme ends, expecting from the great violence of the tempest to part cables every hour, or to drive on shore with our anchors; but thank God, we rode out the gales. Several other vessels were however driven on shore and became wrecks, one under Sandsfoot Castle, others upon the North Shore.'

Further attempts to get Parliamentary approval were made in 1836 and 1840, but behind the scenes plans for organising the vast undertaking were taking shape. Harvey had pointed to 'a great number of poor labourers' the scheme would employ, but nothing short of mobility on a national scale could support work of this magnitude. The solution was to establish a convict 'colony' on Portland, where prisoners sentenced to transportation would quarry the vast quantities of stone required for the breakwater.

It was a select committee of the House of Commons on Shipwrecks which in

1843 finally got things moving. They were aware of the dangers of the Portland Race and West Bay and the lack of any accessible harbour of refuge in storms. A Royal Commission was quickly appointed to consider the question of harbours in Portland Roads and elsewhere.

In 1844 the Hydrographer for the Navy, Admiral Sir Francis Beaufort (he of the scale), asked Commander William Sheringham to make a full survey of the Portland and Weymouth Roads. There was an air of panic as Beaufort wrote 'The sooner you go and the more cheerfully you do the job for this troublesome Harbour Commission the sooner you will be able to return.' Sheringham, who a few years earlier had completed a similar survey of Poole Harbour, duly arrived on his 165-ton wooden paddle steamer HMS *Fearless* to undertake a detailed hydrographic survey, taking soundings of the entire anchorage and measuring its tides and streams.

In May 1844 the 'troublesome' Commissioners for Harbours of Refuge came for themselves, made a minute inspection, and took evidence from local people with knowledge of the sea. They were impressed. Their Report included an enthusiastic recommendation for a breakwater at Portland, and the scheme finally won the determined support of the Prime Minister, Sir Robert Peel.

On 30 July 1845: Viscount Palmerston told Parliament:

'I call the attention of the House to a matter of great national importance, the great imperfection of the present state of our national means of defence. Peace between two countries can never be secure except when they stand upon a footing of equality with regard to their respective means of self-defence.

'The Channel is no longer a barrier. Steam navigation has rendered that which was before impassable by a military force nothing more than a river passable by a steam bridge. France has steamers capable of transporting 30,000 men, and she has harbours, in which these steamers may collect, and around which . . . large bodies of men are constantly quartered. These harbours are directly opposite to our coast, and within a few hours' voyage of the different landing-places on the coast of England.'

The scheme to create a vast harbour from Portland Roads thus moved forward. James Rendel of Plymouth was appointed Engineer-in-Chief for the project, and early in 1846 his team, including Cornish engineer John Coode, surveyed the ground conditions on the site of the proposed incline railway on the north side of the Island.

That August, Queen Victoria and Prince Albert experienced first-hand the need for a breakwater at Portland. Their Royal Yacht, attended by the Admiralty's paddle steamer *Black Eagle*, had to put into the Roads in a storm. It was too rough for the Queen to land, but Captain Charles Augustus Manning of Portland Castle managed to join them aboard. Manning was a highly influential county magistrate, and he accompanied Albert on his several later visits to monitor the progress of the works.

Outline designs for the harbour had already been drawn up in May 1847 when it announced that Royal Assent had been given to the Act of Parliament authorising

The striking figurehead of HMS *Basilisk* stood at the entrance to Portland Naval Base in its latter years. The steam paddler *Basilisk* took part in an historic trial of power with the screwship HMS *Niger* in June 1849. Tied stern to stern in the English Channel, the *Niger* decisively proved the superiority of screw propulsion over paddles.

the scheme. There was much jubilation throughout Dorset. Within weeks the First Lord of the Admiralty, the Right Honourable Earl of Auckland, arrived at the Roads in the HM Steamer *Fire Queen*. He inspected the site of the Breakwater accompanied by Captain Manning.

The Portland Breakwaters eventually created the largest man-made harbour in the world. With its associated defences – the mighty Verne Citadel, the landward gun batteries, the Nothe and Breakwater Forts – it was a national project of monumental scale. During more than half a century this was at times Victorian Britain's biggest and most expensive government funded engineering scheme.

When the Portland Breakwaters were conceived, naval ships were powered by the wind, and steam was still a novelty. Nobody then could imagine the phenomenal changes that science and technology would bring to the maritime world. Neither did anyone contemplate the shifting of the perceived enemy from Spain-France, to Russia then to Germany at the end of the nineteenth century.

The Admiralty's transition from sail to steam was in its initial stages in the mid nineteenth century. Ships at this time were miscellaneous collections of screw-driven, paddle and sailing ships of various speeds and manoeuvrability. Many of their commanding officers were old men, few of them with active service records. The Crimean War (1853-56) led to a radical change in ship design. Initial resistance to the armouring of ships' hulls was overcome when the French proved its efficacy in trials. Screw-driven steamships had now proven far superior to either paddles or sail.

James Rendel drafted his plans for Portland's harbour of refuge in 1846. These showed a straight breakwater projecting in a north-easterly direction from the north-east corner of the island. A gap in the structure (the South Ship Channel) was designed to enable a rapid exit for warships. John Coode amended Rendel's original plan by putting a curve in the outer breakwater arm to turn the construction northwards. The layout allowed three acres per vessel in rough weather, with shelter for 300 large and 150 smaller ships.

The Portland Breakwaters created the largest man-made harbour in the world. The second half of the nineteenth century saw gigantic defences constructed on the Island's Verne Hill (background), at the Nothe, Weymouth and at other locations, all designed to protect British ships from sea-borne attacks.

A big advantage of the Portland anchorage was the small tidal range, some 2 metres at spring tides, direct access to the open sea and a flat seabed unencumbered by rocks.

HM steamship *Driver* made three deliveries of hundreds of convicts for the government works on Portland in late 1848. The convicts were landed and escorted to their new clifftop prison by a detachment of the 23rd Fusiliers and police. *Driver* had made history the year before by being the first steam vessel to circumnavigate the globe. Incidentally, HMS *Driver* brought the author's great-great-grandfather back from the Crimea in 1856.

Within five years Sir John Burgoyne, the Inspector General of Fortifications, believed that the embryo Portland Harbour already afforded good shelter to men-of-war as well as to merchantmen. But 'should there be a war, it is totally without defences.' He proposed that the 'commanding hill of the Verne, above the harbour . . . be converted into a very strong citadel, for its security against attack by land'.

The massive expansion of the Cherbourg naval base had been the focus of fears of invasion of the Dorset coast for 50 years. It is ironic that just as Britain's response, in the form of the great defence works at Portland and Weymouth, was commencing, Napoleon III invited Queen Victoria to open the latest development at Cherbourg, as a gesture of friendship. The ceremony on 5 August, 1858 was magnificent, but the Queen came away dismayed at the prospect of the French Navy becoming more powerful than hers. The Queen let the Prime Minister know in no uncertain terms what she thought of the state of the Royal Navy.

However, as Portland grew in strength and importance, the rapid changes in warfare technology reduced the value of Cherbourg. Many French officers now regarded their great naval base as a trap, indefensible, and unable to protect warships sheltering within it.

By 1851 the benefits of the Portland Breakwater were becoming clear. The winter had seen 130 sail lying in the Roads at one time. A naval captain wrote that in south-west gales much less roll was experienced, although there was not yet enough to shelter large ships from SSE gales. 'I should not hesitate if in command of a line of battleships to receive shelter by anchoring close up to the Breakwater.'

The effectiveness of the works was dramatically demonstrated in January 1851 when 24 sail put in for shelter. When the wind moderated SSE, five sailed off, but the others stayed and shifted their berths to the shelter of the Breakwater. The wind later increased to a gale, and the five that had sailed were either lost or damaged.

The Navy was quick to take advantage of the growing sheltered sector in Portland Roads, even while the Breakwater was only a fraction completed. In late 1854 some one hundred ships anchored there. These included troopships, hospital stores, the French 90-gun sailing ship *Breslau*, and coal vessels, all destined for the Crimea. (France was now an ally of Britain against Russia, but was still regarded as a potential enemy for defensive purposes.)

In 1856 the Lords of the Admiralty arrived at Portland on the *Black Eagle* to inspect the 70-gun screwship HMS *Sans Pareil*, which was accompanied by 41 gunboats, and HMS *Colossus*. The Crimean War had now ended and the *Sans Pareil* was sent to the Baltic to bring home troops. *Colossus* was a fully-rigged 80-

The burgeoning fleets of the Royal Navy were soon making full use of the rapidly developing Portland Harbour, especially as a base for vital training and exercises. Here, HMS *Colossus* is depicted leaving Portland Harbour in April 1856. This impressive fully-rigged sailing ship had been converted to steam screw propulsion before going into action in the Crimean War two years earlier. She dwarfs the accompanying gunboats.

gun sailing ship, being launched in 1848. She was converted to screw propulsion before going into action at the Crimea in 1855. Her later years were spent as the Portland Guard Ship until being broken up in 1867.

Life on board ships of the Royal Navy was changing too. Impressment, compelling men to serve by force and without notice, was last used in 1815, but it was not until 1853 that a Continuous Service scheme was introduced. Young seamen were required to sign on for a 10 year term of pensionable service. Regulation uniforms arrived in 1857, and in 1860 compulsory death sentences were reduced from 10 offences to two – treason and murder. Flogging ceased to be a punishment at the captain's discretion and (officially) ended altogether in the 1870s.

There was resentment on the ships at Portland in December 1859 when officers had orders forbidding them to go ashore unless in uniform. There was stronger anger ashore when it was discovered that naval personnel were instructed not to do business on Portland, but to take their custom to Weymouth shops. One can only speculate what pressure lay behind this.

The Portland Breakwater scheme continued to capture the technical and scientific mind of HRH Prince Albert. He intended a visit in August 1854 to be private, but that was thwarted by national colours being flown at every available building, and on ships. The Prince arrived on the *Victoria and Albert* on a delightfully fine day with a refreshing breeze. A royal gig took him ashore where he inspected the entire structure and closely examined the engineering drawings. He was conveyed in a locomotive truck covered with crimson cloth, accompanied by loud cheers from the assembled crowd. The enthusiastic Prince then walked right to the top of Verne Hill and returned to the Breakwater on the incline railway. As the royal boat left, cheers resounded, ashore and afloat: 'The scene was as charming as the mind could conceive.'

The main Breakwater Fort was an enormous structure and an awesome feat of engineering. Standing in 70 feet of water on a 400 ft wide column of 140,000 tons of granite and limestone, the heavily armed fortress contained officers' quarters, inner court, barrack room, and its own miniature jetty.

In March 1859 the Admiralty gave directions that all newly commissioned ships were to assemble at Portland prior to joining the Channel Squadron. By June of that year the harbour was a scene of activity. Ships were engaged in day-long firing at targets, manning and arming boats, loosing and furling sails; in fact everything required of vessels which ranged from big traditional wooden sailing ships to advanced turreted ironclads.

The Channel Fleet assembled at Portland that summer, and welcomed another visit of Prince Albert with his sons Prince Alfred and Prince Arthur. The steamships included the *Blenheim, James Watt, Exmouth, Hero, Mersey, Cressy, Algiers* and the *Royal Albert*. Exercising and offshore target practice continued apace.

An unusual trial took place in September 1859. Engineer John Coode needed to know whether to use granite or Portland stone for the Inner Fort on the Breakwater.

The gigantic Admiralty floating dock *Bermuda* was one of the strangest craft to come to Dorset for trials, before leaving Portland for Bermuda in 1869. She was towed to Madeira by HMS *Northumberland* and HMS *Agincourt*. *Warrior* and *Black Prince* completed the tow to Bermuda.

The army built butt walls of each type of stone, and HMS *Blenheim* pounded them with heavy fire from a range of 450 yards. The granite shattered, and Portland stone was chosen. Throughout this time the defence works on the Nothe Fort and at Portland were progressing rapidly. Moorings were laid down alongside the Breakwater jetty to facilitate the coaling of a line of battleships.

Rapid changes were taking place in the propulsion of naval ships, but in 1860 steam was still auxiliary to sail. Marine steam engines were as yet inefficient, and the first steam battlefleet, and the subsequent ironclads were, for much of their sea-time, sailing ships assisted by steam.

The British Navy then had 518 vessels, of which 314 were in commission and doing duty in every part of the globe. Of the 65 line-of-battle ships, frigates, sloops, and gunboats, 19 were attached to the Channel Squadron which was frequently at Portland. Its Commander-in-Chief was Rear-Admiral Sir Charles Fremantle on the large wooden battleship *Royal Albert*, with its crew of 1050 men.

July 1860 saw the splendid spectacle of 11 large men-of-war under full sail cruising round the Island. The ships were all veterans of the Baltic expedition: the *Colossus, Majestic, Blenheim, Ajax, Hogue, Cornwallis, Hawke, Dauntless, Pembroke, Edinburgh* and *Russell*. On leaving the harbour the two latter vessels, had to be assisted round the end of the outer Breakwater by the steam tug *Rattler*.

The epoch of the iron-hulled steamship arrived with the launching in 1860 of HMS *Warrior*. With her, the British roundly trumped France's new but smaller and less powerful *La Gloire*, the first ocean-going ironclad battleship. The revolutionary *Warrior* was a frequent visitor to Portland in the 1860s. She was Portsmouth-based but most years she was in Dorset for extended periods. *Warrior* had a huge appetite for coal, and Portland struggled to provide her, especially as the 4000 ton

Behind the training ship *Boscawen* lies the famous *Warrior*. At her launch in 1861 she was the pride of the Navy. Fourteen years later she was relegated to Portland's Coastguard ship, overtaken by rapid technological change. This revolutionary vessel is preserved at Portsmouth.

capacity Great Coaling Shed had proved impracticable.

By the date of Prince Albert's visit in 1861 the cavernous dry moat around the Verne Citadel was nearly complete. Entering the citadel from a high gangway the Prince was startled by a deafening roar from hundreds of workmen. Millions of bricks, forty thousand tons of stone 'enough to build a 35ft square column 500ft high' had already been used in the tunnels, barracks and buildings on the hilltop above the harbour. Four months after his energetic climb over Portland's heights in the searing heat of the sun, Prince Albert was dead. He died just three days after the last pile for the Breakwater had been driven. Only after his death did Dorset learn how deep had been his involvement behind the scenes. *The Times* (January 1863) reported that it was 'due to his enlightened judgement that the Breakwater project was undertaken.'

Local newspapers enthused over the ironclads in Portland Roads, as in March 1864: 'Not in any other part of this great empire can be seen a greater combination of engineering achievements. They can now be seen in one small focus from Portland Roads'. Nobody could fail to be impressed by the scale of the great Breakwater; the Verne fortress; the fort under construction on the Nothe; the great naval vessels such as the sister vessels *Warrior* and *Black Prince*, the *Prince Consort* and *Defence*.

Portland's Coastguard ship, HMS *Royal Alfred*, was replaced in 1875 by the famous HMS *Warrior*. At her launch only 14 years before, *Warrior* was by far the largest, fastest, and most heavily-armoured warship ever, but she was already outdated. Just six years separated her from HMS *Bellerophon*, the first RN ship to carry a balanced rudder. It took forty men 90 seconds to apply full helm on *Warrior*; the same on *Bellerophon* took only eight men just 27 seconds. Innovation was rapid and in 1877 local people were mesmerised as they watched scintillating night tests, when warships in the harbour including *Warrior* were fitted with electric lighting.

FIVE

A NEW BASE

The twin 1.6 mile long Breakwaters sheltered the largest man-made harbour in the world, some 2130 acres. John Coode was knighted, and in August 1872 the Prince of Wales arrived to formally declare the works complete. The Channel and Reserve Squadrons assembled in the harbour, headed by 15 huge ironclads, including *Minotaur*, *Agincourt*, *Achilles* and *Hercules*. Also present were *Northumberland*, *Black Prince*, *Hector*, *Valiant*, *Bellerophon*, *Hercules*, *Vanguard*, *Audacious*, *Sultan* and *Penelope*, *Resistance* and the ironclad steam corvette *Favorite*. The day was blustery which probably accounted for young William Andrews falling to his death from *Bellerophon*'s yardarm. Amid royal salutes, the Prince of Wales arrived aboard the *Victoria and Albert*, to perform the ceremony of laying the last stone. After the State Barge brought him ashore, the Portland Artillery Band struck up in front of the Admiralty Offices, and children sang 'God Bless the Prince of Wales' on the grass banks above.

Portland now had a world class anchorage where soon up to 200 ships at a time could be accommodated. It had a larger area of deep water than any other harbour in Great Britain.

Throughout that period visitors were often welcomed aboard to inspect the huge guns and engines of the latest vessels, such as the turret ship HMS *Thunderer* (1872). She was sister ship to the twin screw turret ship HMS *Devastation*, a prototype of the twentieth century battleship and the Navy's first capital ship with no rigging. She had one short mast for signalling purposes, and her hull was

HMS *Devastation* was the Navy's first capital ship with no rigging. Straight after commissioning in 1873 she came to Portland for trials, including rolling sea tests, broadside to wind and waves. The iconic image of *Devastation* featured on the famous 'England's Glory' matchboxes.

Pre-Dreadnought Majestic Class battleships at anchor at Portland around 1898. They were distinguished by having funnels two abreast instead of the usual fore and aft. They also had advanced uniform protective armour unlike their predecessors which had a thickened steel belt around the hull midriff. Beyond is a line of twelve 'dolphins' (wooden staging on piles), a temporary defence pending the construction of the last breakwaters.

shielded with up to 12 inches of armour.

The turret ship HMS *Glatton* was involved in an unusual firing trial in 1873. She was securely anchored fore and aft as a 'living' target for the ironclad *Hotspur*, which incidentally had a heavy ram fitted on her bow. The latter's heavy gun fired directly at *Glatton's* turret to test its ability to withstand shell impact; the damage was manageable. As with many late nineteenth century naval events in this area, this was featured in national publications such as *The Illustrated London News*.

The late Victorian Royal Navy had little experience of real conflict. This 1896 drill for repelling borders with swords and wooden bats strikes a contrast with the ship's great guns.

A study of mid-Victorian naval architecture: Nearest here in 1873 is the training ship HMS *Boscawen*, originally HMS *Trafalgar* launched in 1841. Next is the Portland Guardship HMS *Achilles* an iron screwship of improved design based on HMS *Warrior*. Behind is HMS *Minotaur* of 1868, the one-time Flagship of the Channel Squadron. *Minotaur* eventually joined *Boscawen* as a training ship in 1893.

In November 1885 onlookers gathered on the hill overlooking the extreme tip of Portland Bill to watch a spectacular experiment. A dummy retractable gun had been mounted on a revolutionary Moncrieff retractable carriage in a purpose-built dugout, and HMS *Hercules* was briefed to open fire with everything she had to destroy it. The gun was exposed for only 20 seconds before ducking below ground, and *Hercules* failed to score. The disappearing gun carriage was thereafter widely installed across the world.

Portland had now become indispensable for the Royal Navy. The Admiralty regarded it as 'One of the most important places in the United Kingdom for our battleships,' and the Dorset coast was regularly used for naval manoeuvres, trials and exercises in late Victorian times. The big ironclads frequenting the harbour in the 1880s carried some of the heaviest guns ever mounted at sea.

In January 1862 *The Times* announced that the Training Ship *Britannia* (formerly *Prince of Wales*), 'the nursery for our future admirals', had arrived at Portland. After 3 years she was transferred to Dartmouth, which later won a battle with Portland for the prestigious Naval College. In October 1866 *Britannia*'s moorings at Portland were taken by HMS *Boscawen*, a three decked sailing ship of the line, launched in 1844. She had seen action in the Crimea in 1855, but reduced to a hulk before being restored as a training ship for boy seamen. Lads keen to join the Navy had to be 14 – 16 years old and over a minimum height and chest size, 'able to read and write fairly, be strong, healthy, well-grown, active, intelligent, free from all physical malformation, and must never have had fits'.

The 500 boys on *Boscawen* were pushed to their limits, but training had not caught up with the age of steam and the ironclads; initially it still reflected life at sea under

31

Thousands of boys every year underwent their sea training in the *Boscawen* and the other training ships at Portland. They got a full education with vigorous grounding in seamanship. These youngsters look happy enough here on Castletown beach, but punishments sometimes got out of hand. Flogging was common, sometimes with birch pickled in brine. An overly harsh regime and rotting timbers contributed to the removal of *Boscawen* in 1905.

sail. Climbing to the topmast to set rigging took nerve for a 14-year-old. They had conventional lessons, and undertook every describable chore including cooking and scrubbing their hammocks on deck. In their spare time they had to do physical drill, weight lifting and gymnastics, and rifle drill. Ten years later the boys of the by then

Boscawen boys scrubbing their hammocks.

Seaflower, the Royal Navy's last sail training brig.

ageing *Boscawen* were transferred to the even older HMS *Trafalgar*, one of the 'wooden walls of old England' now back in her familiar waters. The name *Boscawen* was transferred to the *Trafalgar*.

Ships' crews were often exercised ashore, as in October 1877, when 1000 fully armed seamen of the Channel Squadron under the command of Admiral Dowell, 'accompanied by their respective bands and a battery of field pieces, and an ambulance party were landed and marched to the naval Cadets Recreation ground, where various field evolutions were gone through'. 'The battalions having marched past in review order, a sham fight followed which continued until noon. The weather was beautifully fine; several hundred spectators witnessed the proceedings from the grassy slopes overlooking the ground.'

The large Cadets' and Officers' recreation grounds near Portland's Victoria Square, originally public common lands, were upgraded to full sports fields in 1905 and used extensively by the Navy and others until 1995. Those irreplaceable fields were built upon in 2011.

The last sailing ship built for the Royal Navy was the training brig *Seaflower* which was launched in 1873. She arrived at Portland in 1879 along with the brig *Martin* as tenders for the *Boscawen*.

In 1893 TS *Boscawen* was joined at her Portland moorings by HMS *Agincourt* and her sister ship *Minotaur*. Both had been frequent visitors to Portland and were prominent when the Prince of Wales laid the ceremonial stone to mark the completion of the Breakwater in 1872. As the faded *Agincourt* lay stationary in the harbour for 12 years, few may have remembered that during her active career she was the flagship of no less than fifteen admirals, some of whom were among the most notable figures of Victorian naval history.

The *Minotaur* (1863) too had a distinguished service. From 1867 she was the

Top Home comforts in the Captain's Cabin aboard HMS *Theseus* in 1897. The captain could summons his subordinates with the chain bell-pulls hanging above him.

Above Polished efficiency and strict discipline, gun training in 1898.

flagship of the Channel Fleet, and served the Navy in various roles for nearly 60 years.

On conversion to training ships *Minotaur* and *Agincourt* were renamed *Boscawen II* and *III* respectively. The three old *Boscawen*s were seemingly permanent fixtures in the Harbour for many years. They had imparted sea skills to thousands of youths who trod their decks. However, following allegations about birching and brutal treatment aboard, the ships were removed 'to make room for the Fleet' in 1905 – a great loss to Portland and Weymouth traders.

SIX

UNDERSEA PERIL

Nothing had a more profound effect on naval warfare than the development of the torpedo. Robert Whitehead was already a successful mechanical engineer when in 1866 he produced a prototype torpedo propelled by compressed air. The Admiralty saw the potential, but decreed that the Royal Navy would only acquire torpedoes made in this country. Eventually a greenfield site at Wyke Regis on the north-west shore of Portland Harbour was found to be the ideal location for his new factory, which opened in 1891. A long pier was constructed from the factory into the harbour for torpedo trials, a 1500 yards range was established, and a second 3000 yards range followed near Bincleaves for the Admiralty. These ranges caused problems for commercial shipping; there were many accidents, as in 1904 when a Norwegian freighter was hit by a torpedo (fortunately with no explosive) whist crossing the zone.

With orders from many foreign countries, Whitehead and his family became wealthy. One granddaughter, Marguerite Hoyos, married the son of Herbert von Bismarck, of the noble German family. In 1912 another granddaughter, Agatha Whitehead, married a distinguished Austrian submarine commander, Captain

Robert Whitehead established the first torpedo works on the Wyke Regis shore of Portland Harbour in 1891. The formidable weapon was soon adopted by navies, friend and foe. With gyroscopic stabilizing devices and compressed air engines, by 1900 the torpedo attained speeds of 28 knots and a range of 1000 yards.

Georg von Trapp (their children became immortalised in 'The Sound of Music').

The first battleship to be fitted with torpedo tubes was HMS *Inflexible* of 1876. As early as 1882 torpedo instruction for boys was being given at a new shore training establishment on the eastern slopes of Portland, an adjunct of HMS *Boscawen*. A depot was set up in the dockyard to service torpedoes from the fleet. This was later moved across the harbour to Bincleaves.

It is ironic that with torpedoes being made on one side of the harbour, on the opposite, eastern side the long gap between the Breakwater Fort and Bincleaves on the Weymouth shore was completely open to enemy assault by the new weapon. Under cover of darkness, new light torpedo boats could approach at high speed from the south-east and attack ships lying at their moorings.

The first real 'torpedo boat destroyers', the *Havok* and *Hornet* of 1893, attained world record speeds of 27 knots. Unfortunately they were faster than their bow-launched torpedoes! The steam turbine *Viper* torpedo boat destroyer of 1898 was even faster. The development of the torpedo undermined previous notions of the defence of ships in port. It was a new and deadly potential threat to the hundreds of warships and merchantmen frequenting the harbour. There was only one solution for Portland; a physical barrier had to be built across the two mile gap between the Breakwater Fort and the Weymouth shore at Bincleaves.

A scheme was drawn up and the go-ahead was given in 1894 for the work to be done by convict and direct labour. In 1895 the government signed a contract with a Portland company, Stewards, for the supply of 2 million tons of rough stone. Three years later the whole job was handed over to Hill & Co of Gosport.

The full enclosure of the harbour was needed urgently, and could not await the estimated ten year construction period, so twelve artificial islands (dolphins) were first constructed, 6-800 yards apart, between which anti-submarine cables were to be strung. However, these provided no protection against attack by torpedoes, or against bad weather.

On the Portland side, the original coaling jetty (later nicknamed 'Monkey Island') with its elaborate handling mechanisms had been a disastrous mistake. It should have done away with lighters and colliers, but when completed it was found that the tipped stone foundations prevented large ships getting close. This was an embarrassment since Portland was now the Navy's principal coaling station, and was to be home to the Channel Fleet.

In March 1903 a contract was let for a new coaling pier, to be fitted with gigantic hydraulic machinery. This was completed in 1907, but again technology had overtaken events. Fuel storage was now needed for the new oil-powered ships, so a range of big fuel tanks was planned at the Mere, near the south-west corner of the harbour. When the first tanks were erected in 1905 local wits said the cylindrical monsters were to hold the Navy's grog! Progress into the twentieth century accelerated with the building of an electric power station at Castletown in 1906 to supply the naval base.

The torpedo changed the nature of sea warfare almost overnight. The Dorset anchorage was completely open to enemy assault by the new weapon. The solution was to close the gap between the Breakwater Fort and Bincleaves with two new breakwaters. Stone for the work was loaded at a special jetty, seen here in about 1898.

The new Northern Breakwater joined the Weymouth shore at Bincleaves. The Admiralty took over land there which had been reclaimed by the Great Western Railway Company for an aborted commercial docks scheme, and this became the site of the Bincleaves Torpedo Testing Establishment. A lighthouse was erected on the outer head, by the new East Ship Channel opposite the Breakwater Fort, in 1905. After more than half a century, the four-mile string of breakwaters was thus finally complete.

By the turn of the twentieth century all the grandiose and expensive defences built in south Dorset since Palmerston's days had become obsolete with the advent of torpedoes, submarines, and impending aircraft.

The first British submarine was launched in November 1901, and three years later ships from Portland took part in a mock war against submarines. The countermeasures then consisted of a large mesh net which had to be spread between destroyers and battleships on sighting the periscope of an approaching submarine. When the submarines 'sank' four of the ships it dawned on the Admiralty that they were a force to be reckoned with.

The brief nine-year Edwardian period was a time of phenomenal change, with the rapid progression in the design and production of British submarines, warships and aircraft. Within three years of a surprise visit by Edward VII in 1902 the sight of naval ships with black hulls, white upperworks and yellow funnels was a thing of the past: from 1905 the naval livery was battleship grey.

BRITAIN'S BULWARKS
A SUBMARINE OF "C" CLASS.

A 'C' Class submarine in about 1908. The Admiralty took some convincing that they were a useful weapon of war, but by 1912 Britain had more submarines than any other nation.

Portland Harbour was now a hub of naval activity. Some 180 warships and 85 torpedo boat destroyers used the local facilities in 1907. Ships were drilled in anti-torpedo routines, 'darkening ship', collision stations, coaling, maintenance and gunnery. Torpedo boat destroyers were organized into flotillas of up to 20 boats which were herded into 'pens', special jetties which had been constructed near Castletown. Conditions on board them were cramped, so the crews were given special concessions; their 'tot' of rum was issued neat, instead of being watered down as was the regulation.

Lord Charles Beresford hoisted his C-in-C flag on HMS *King Edward VII* at Portland on 16 April 1907. Under his command the Channel Fleet comprised 14 battleships, four armoured cruisers, two second class cruisers and one third class cruiser. In time of war it was planned that Beresford would be given supreme command over all 244 fighting vessels of the Navy. However this

A remarkable 1907 photograph of Lord Charles Beresford (centre) with Admiral Percy Scott (right) apparently in good spirits after giving a pep-talk at the new Fleet Canteen, Castletown. Beresford commanded the Channel Fleet, based at Portland. Scott and Beresford were intense rivals, frequently at loggerheads over operational strategies.

The vast harbour filled almost to capacity with the Channel Fleet. Elegant Admiralty steam yachts conveyed the naval hierarchy around the warships. The power station (right) of 1906 provided electricity to the base, 23 years before the civilians had a supply.

was peacetime and there were three Commanders-in-Chief in home waters; a recipe for friction and personality clashes at the top. In one incident the cruiser *Good Hope* was undertaking gunnery practice off Lulworth Cove when Beresford ordered it back to harbour for sprucing up for a visit of the Kaiser. Rear Admiral Sir Percy Scott on *Good Hope* relayed the curt signal: 'As paintwork appears to be more important than gunnery you are to return to harbour to make yourselves look pretty'. Beresford was livid.

When thousands of sailors were in port they naturally took their custom – and their thirst – ashore. At one time Portland claimed to have had more pubs per head of population than anywhere else in England, an anomaly in a staunchly

Through the early twentieth century the Navy took every opportunity to parade through the streets of Portland and Weymouth.

Methodist island! A moral dimension was added by the famous Aggie Weston who opened a coffee shop for sailors at Victoria Square, Portland, in 1880, followed by Royal Sailors' Rest Homes in both Weymouth and Portland. The Salvation Army built a large (strictly teetotal) hostel in 1920 at Castletown, then a bustling one-street 'town' which developed entirely on the strength of naval patronage.

Weymouth, where there was plenty of entertainment, was always the main attraction for sailors ashore. A large Royal Sailors Home (later the White Ensign Club) opened in St Nicholas Street.

Intense firing exercises by the new big-gunned battleships were now causing noise and vibration ashore. Complaints from villages along the Dorset coast and even from Bournemouth were dismissed with little sympathy by the Admiralty.

An action packed three days awaited George V at Weymouth and Portland in May 1912. The king arrived on the *Victoria and Albert* with his naval cadet son, Prince Albert (later George VI), along with the First Lord of the Admiralty, Winston Churchill; Prime Minister Herbert Asquith, and Second Sea Lord, Admiral Prince Louis of Battenberg. They witnessed a spectacular array of Britain's greatest warships. Assembled for the Naval Review in six lines were 28 battleships, 3 battlecruisers, 11 heavy cruisers, 7 flotillas of 33-knot destroyers and nearly 50 submarines.

In the Channel off Portland they watched mock submarine attacks, ships' firing practice and pioneering aerial displays. The party first went to Weymouth, which was ablaze with bunting from end to end, and sightseers by the thousand had come on steamers and trains. They were mesmerised by the aerobatics, and startled when Lt. Gregory dropped a 300 lb iron dummy bomb close to the king's

A youthful Prince Albert (later King George VI) on HMS *Neptune* at Portland. His father George V is on the left. The cadet prince joined *HMS Collingwood* in 1913 and served as a midshipman in the Great War.

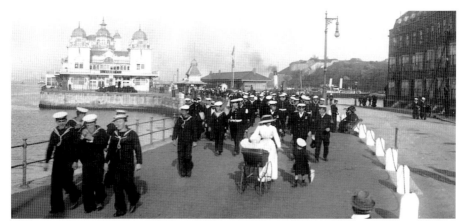

The nightlife, pubs – and girls – of Weymouth were irresistible magnets for sailors. The town overflowed with bluejackets when the fleets were in harbour.

Welfare and hospitality was important for time ashore. A magnificent Royal Sailors Home (later the White Ensign Club) opened in Weymouth in 1907. A popular 'home' at Queens Road, Portland, catered also for soldiers stationed at the Verne Citadel. This was bombed in the Second World War with serious loss of life.

Sailors returning to their ship from Weymouth on the paddle steamer *Albert Victor* in around 1911.

A naive painting, later issued as a postcard, showing the Combined British Fleets assembled in Weymouth Bay for the Naval Review at Weymouth, May 1912. With the king on the royal yacht (shown centre right) were Winston Churchill, then First Lord of the Admiralty, and Prime Minister Asquith.

yacht near the harbour entrance. The king later became the first royal to venture underwater in a submarine, the new *D4*. It cruised at periscope depth, and surfaced in thick fog.

The pre-Dreadnought *Hibernia* had been fitted with a launching platform, and arrived with four planes on board. Commander Charles Samson took off in his Short S.27 biplane from the *Hibernia* steaming at 10.5 knots. This was the first ever successful take-off from a moving ship at sea. Landing on a moving ship had yet to

be attempted so he came down on a grass 'airstrip' at Lodmoor, Weymouth. Other flights by Samson, and Commander Jerrard, Lieutenants Longmore and Gregory followed. Some of the flimsy aircraft, the hydro-aeroplanes – were fitted

One of the ships to take part in the Review of 1912 was the *Dreadnought*. It was launched in 1906, and with its ten 12-inch guns, displacement of 18,000 tons and a speed of 21 knots, there was nothing at sea to match it.

In May 1912, from HMS *Hibernia* steaming off Portland at 15.5 knots, Commander Charles Samson took off in his Short S.27 biplane, the first ever successful take-off from a moving ship at sea.

A flimsy hydro-aeroplane with airbag floats returns to the slipway at Portland.

with airbag floats for landing on water. On one flight Samson took an admiral's daughter up as a passenger. 29 year-old Samson was described as 'a little short man with a real naval beard and a fine flow of language', but he proved himself a superb aviator. His colleague Arthur Longmore was in 1914 the first to test the dropping of torpedoes from aircraft, and went on to win a knighthood and become an RAF Air Chief Marshal.

The Royal Flying Corps had been established only three weeks before the Royal Review. Two years later, at Churchill's instigation a Naval Wing of the Royal Flying Corps was formed, to be known as The Royal Naval Air Service. This came under the full control of the Royal Navy in 1915.

SEVEN

THE NAVY GOES TO WAR

Anglo-German relations had been deteriorating since the turn of the twentieth century. Under First Sea Lord, Sir John Fisher, 'a volcanic genius of the highest order', ship design was revolutionised; gunfire range increased from 3000 to 10,000 yards, and in 1906 the powerful *Dreadnought* was launched. With its ten 12-inch guns, displacement of 18,000 tons and a speed of 21 knots, there was nothing at sea to match it. The megalomaniac Kaiser Wilhelm II was furious, and the Germans responded by ratcheting up their ship design and construction to unprecedented levels. The outcome of this naval arms race quickly became apparent when war was declared on August 4 1914. A month earlier, the 460 ships of the Home Fleets gathered at Portland. Churchill later recollected: 'It constituted incomparably the greatest assemblage of naval power ever assembled in the history of the world'.

Churchill soon realised that such a concentration of warships at Portland presented a tempting target for a pre-emptive strike by German destroyers. On his own volition Churchill ordered the First Fleet [later the Grand Fleet] 'to sail secretly tomorrow for its preliminary Northern station'. Nobody except flag and commanding officers was to be told of the destination. The fleet set sail for Scapa Flow and Rosyth at 07:00 on 29 July 1914.

In his masterly turn of phrase Churchill later recalled:

'We may now picture this great Fleet, with its flotillas and cruisers, steaming slowly out of Portland Harbour, squadron by squadron, scores of gigantic castles of steel wending their way across the misty, shining sea, like giants bowed in

The destroyer HMS *Fawn* at Portland shortly after the outbreak of the First World War.

HMS *Hood* in its heyday. The Channel Fleet, with 26 battleships moored in its Portland base, was vulnerable to submarine attack. The photograph below shows the 23-year-old battleship in position prior to being scuttled to block the South Ship Channel of the Breakwater.

anxious thought. We may picture them again as darkness fell, eighteen miles of warships running at high speed and in absolute blackness through the narrow Straits, bearing with them into the broad waters of the North the safeguard of considerable affairs . . . The King's ships were at sea.'

The Portland based Channel Fleet alone now included 26 battleships, 9 cruisers and 4 light cruisers. In November 1914 it was reinforced by the 3rd Battle Squadron with its flagship *King Edward VII* in response to German naval activity in the Channel Fleet's area.

On 4 November the redundant battleship HMS *Hood* was scuttled to block the South Ship Channel, the original gap in the Breakwater, to prevent enemy submarines and torpedoes attacking through it. The Naval hierarchy had finally conceded that some local experts were right when in 1847 they challenged the

ROYAL NAVAL DIVISION
HANDYMEN TO FIGHT ON LAND & SEA

1ST BRIGADE	2ND BRIGADE
BATTALIONS:	BATTALIONS:
"BENBOW"	"HOWE"
"COLLINGWOOD"	"HOOD"
"HAWKE"	"ANSON"
"DRAKE"	"NELSON"
RECRUITS WANTED	RECRUITS WANTED

VACANCIES FOR RECRUITS BETWEEN THE AGES OF **18** AND **38**
CHEST MEASUREMENT. 34   HEIGHT. 5 FT. 3½ IN.
PAYMENT from 1/3 per day. **FAMILY ALLOWANCES**
Besides serving in the above Battalions and for the Transport and Engineer Sections attached.
MEN WANTED
who are suitable for Training as Wireless Operators, Signalmen and other Service with the Fleet.

Above The poet Rupert Brooke at Blandford Camp.

Top left Recruiting poster for the Royal Naval Division, whose base was established at Blandford.

Centre left A Royal Naval Division ambulance.

Below left George V and Winston Churchill, then First Lord of the Admiralty, arriving at Blandford to inspect the Royal Naval Division before it set sail for the ill-fated Gallipoli campaign in 1915.

The cruiser HMS *Roxburgh* in Weymouth Bay in 1914. Despite predating the Dreadnought class, she served in, and survived, the war.

At the outbreak of the war HMS *Marlborough* was the first vessel to be fitted with anti-aircraft guns. She was damaged in a torpedo attack at the Battle of Jutland, and while in the Black Sea in 1919 rescued some members of the Russian Imperial Family.

original concept for a gap there.

Such was the enthusiasm to fight for the country the Navy found itself with far more reservist volunteers than they had ships for. In August 1914 the Admiralty formed the Royal Naval Division (RND), establishing its training base at Blandford, and naming its battalions after famous naval officers: Drake, Nelson, Benbow, Hawke, Hood, Howe, Anson and Collingwood. The camp was built quickly with its own church, hospital, canteen and railway line and station.

One officer based in Blandford was Rupert Brooke, probably the most famous poet of his time, who penned these memorable words:

'If I should die, think only this of me:
That there's some corner of a foreign field
That is for ever England . . .'

Brooke did die, at only 27 – from a septic mosquito bite – one of 141,029 Allied casualties at the ill-fated Gallipoli campaign against the Turks. His memory lives on in his prolific and moving poetry which instilled a modicum of comfort to countless grief-stricken families at home.

Seven hundred sailors of the Collingwood Battalion from RND Blandford landed

BRITAIN'S BULWARKS
H M S "FORMIDABLE"

In a rough sea west of Portland Bill a solitary German submarine, the *U-24*, launched a deadly torpedo attack on HMS *Formidable*. It was New Year's Eve 1914, and 547 of her crew perished. Below is a rare German postcard showing an artist's impression of the sinking.

Das englische Linienschiff „FORMIDABLE"
wurde am 1. Januar 1915
durch ein deutsches Unterseeboot zum Sinken gebracht.

at Cape Helles in May 1915. In their attack in the Battle of Krithia on 4 June they were caught out by devastating flanking fire, which killed or wounded more than 500 men. The survivors withdrew but so heavy were the casualties that the Battalion could not be reformed. A memorial to this unique Dorset naval infantry stands at Collingwood Corner on the Salisbury to Blandford Road.

Another early casualty of the war was the battleship HMS *Ocean*, which hit a mine and sank in 1915. Here some of the crew are lined up for inspection in Castletown.

Meanwhile at sea the U-boat rapidly proved to be Germany's most dangerous weapon. The Great War brought serious merchant and naval losses off the Dorset coast. Huge numbers of smaller craft had to be diverted to patrol duties. An early casualty was HMS *Formidable*, which having proudly served in the Mediterranean Fleet, Channel, Home and Atlantic Fleets, was again with the Channel Fleet when she entered war service. On New Year's Eve 1914 west of Portland Bill, the sea was rough with the wind increasing, and she had just completed a gunnery exercise with the Battle Squadron. In heavy seas, a solitary German submarine, the *U*-24 launched a torpedo which struck home. After midnight and with a heavy list Captain Noel Loxley ordered the crew to abandon ship. Sea conditions were now atrocious and in the blackness several of the ship's boats were smashed. At 3:05 *Formidable* was struck by a second torpedo, and despite a heroic rescue of 233 of the crew, many of whom landed at Lyme Regis, 547 of their fellows, including Captain Loxley were lost.

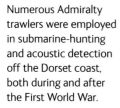

Numerous Admiralty trawlers were employed in submarine-hunting and acoustic detection off the Dorset coast, both during and after the First World War.

The *Formidable* was one of the first British battleships to be sunk during the First World War. Her loss made the Admiralty wary of allowing the 5th Battle Fleet to leave Portland Harbour, but it eventually sailed at the end of January 1915.

Portland Harbour was formally designated a war anchorage and trawler station under the control of the Portland Command area. More than 60 drifters and trawlers arrived to be fitted out for minesweeping, and later they were joined by motor launches based in Weymouth.

Throughout 1916 and 1917 German U-boats continued to lay mines off the Dorset coast. By the end of 1916 U-boats had sunk over 2 million tons of British merchant shipping besides 24 warships. Portland-based minesweepers had to constantly sweep a wide channel to keep a clear path through Weymouth Bay and the Portland approaches. The trawler-based minesweepers at Portland were later augmented by the 17th Fleet Minesweeping Flotilla comprising a few converted paddle steamers. At times more than 200 armed trawlers were based in the harbour.

On 30 April 1917 the minesweeping trawler *Arfon* stuck a mine and exploded off St Alban's Head with the loss of 10 men. Numerous mines were swept and destroyed including some near the Shambles lightship, off Anvil Point and in West Bay where the dredger *St Dunstan* met a similar fate that September.

In the heat of war there were many accidents. In January 1918 the submarine depot ship HMS *Hazard* was cruising off Dorset when she was rammed by a hospital ship, the SS *Western Australia*. The latter managed to rescue her crew. On the seabed the *Hazard* joined submarine A3, with which she had collided six years earlier. The A3 went down off the Isle of Wight with all her crew of 14, but in May 1912 the sub was raised and sunk again as a gunnery target off Portland Bill.

Cordite was a low-explosive propellant which replaced gunpowder, and from the 1890s was extensively used in naval guns and rifles. Winston Churchill, the First Lord of the Admiralty, now insisted that the Royal Navy had its own independent supply of cordite, and an isolated but accessible site was selected for

The sloop HMS *Heather*, a disguised armed Q-ship in the war, later became a centre for hydrophone submarine detection training in Portland Harbour.

50

HMS *Iron Duke* flying the flag of Admiral Jellicoe in the Great War. As First Sea Lord, Jellicoe initiated urgent anti-submarine research which became centred on Portland.

the RN Cordite Factory (RNCF) at Holton Heath, Dorset. A special railway siding and a water reservoir were constructed, and a jetty was built in Poole Harbour near the main site. The existence of this unusual naval site was kept a close secret throughout its existence, although up to 4,500 people worked there. To create the large quantities of acetone needed for the production of cordite, grain was fermented, but when in 1917 grain became in short supply, local schoolchildren were recruited to collect horse chestnuts as a substitute!

With such a volatile substance accidents were inevitable. The worst tragedy was on 23 June 1931 when a nitro-glycerine compound became unstable and a huge explosion in one of the laboratories killed 10 men and injured 19.

As the war progressed the British realised that the German High Seas Fleet based near Heligoland could probably destroy any ship in the Channel. It could assemble at least 13 dreadnoughts, a large number of armoured cruisers, and hundreds of destroyers to attack shipping in the Channel. As much of the Royal Navy was now in the North Sea, all that could be mustered to defend the Channel were some old lightly armed cruisers that had been incapable of joining the big, fast dreadnoughts of the Grand Fleet in Scapa Flow.

The departure of the fleets for the Orkneys had left Dorset waters deceptively peaceful. The situation for merchant shipping everywhere was desperate, as one out of every four vessels leaving UK ports was sunk. Merchant vessels were routed along selected approaches, but these were inadequately guarded and the Germans soon learned the supposedly secret courses. They became death-traps in which a U-boat only had to wait for the approach of its victims.

The catastrophic losses by U-boats caused even non-mariners to come up with desperate solutions. Before 1914 all the anti-submarine efforts were mechanical,

51

and often farcical: lassoing periscopes and sliding a grenade down the wire; using towed grapples with dangling charges, and even lassoing the whole submarine with a noose of explosives. The author's grandfather wrote to the Admiralty Board of Invention and Research on 16 December 1917 detailing his idea for vessels to be fitted with a retractable frame surrounding surface warships hulls with screens of steel hawsers 'of such elasticity that the contact of the torpedo would cause it to rebound without exploding'. The Board considered many bizarre ideas for locating submarines, involving sea lions, seagulls, and even effervescent bubbles. There were reports that some trawlers were issued with bags and sledge hammers, for putting over and smashing enemy periscopes! However it was science that was eventually to match the menace.

The use of hydrophones to detect submerged submarines by listening was first contemplated in 1914. Two years into the war hydrophones were still in their infancy, and depth charges – the most effective device – were in short supply. The difficulty of destroying submarines meant that only seven U-boats were sunk in over 100 engagements in 1916. In response to scathing accusations of Admiralty incompetence and inertia, Admiral Jellicoe, the newly appointed First Sea Lord, convened the Anti-Submarine Detection Committee to concentrate efforts. Researchers investigated using quartz piezoelectric sensors to convert the reflected sound waves into electricity and developed the concept of underwater sound echo-location. The result was ASDIC, later to be manifested as Sonar.

In 1917 the Admiralty's anti-submarine strategy became centred on Dorset, and following a temporary set-up in Weymouth, a shore establishment was built on Portland. Commissioned as HMS *Sarepta*, it was closed briefly after the Armistice in November 1918, but re-opened soon after. On this East Weares site, training for officers and ratings was combined with experimental work to develop hydrophones, ASDIC and other submarine detection devices. The 20 year-old battleships *Implacable* and *Venerable* were brought in as mother ships for the numerous trawlers which worked up their sub-hunting and acoustic detection skills at sea.

After training the vessels were sent into action. The new detection systems and the introduction of convoys changed the course of the war at sea. Among the U-boats destroyed in the Channel off Dorset were submarines *UB-74*, *UC-51*, *UB-54*, *UB-19*, *UC-62*, *UB-72*, *U-85*, *UB-74* and *UB-17*, and the number of merchant ships lost was drastically reduced. Over the next 70 years the research and training establishment on Portland developed into a huge organisation at the forefront of torpedo and submarine detection science.

The first flying machine to touch local soil had been the Short 41 hydro-aeroplane, in 1912. 'HMS *Amphibian*' as it was named, was housed in a shed above a converted boat slip on the southern shore of Portland Harbour. In September 1916 the Royal Naval Air Service set up a seaplane base there and a purpose-built hangar was erected. Initially No. 241 Squadron had two flights equipped with several Short

The British Grand Fleet in 1918.

225 and 240 seaplanes for anti-submarine patrols along the English Channel. The base was part of HMS *Sarepta* and also had Admiralty Type 184 Shorts, which had been the first aircraft in the world to sink an enemy ship with a torpedo.

From 1916 onwards the RNAS also established a number of small coastal aerodromes for use by short-range anti-submarine aircraft. One of these was at Chickerell near Weymouth which opened in 1918. The flights were equipped with de Havilland DH 6 patrol aircraft, given the nicknames 'The Crab' or the 'Flying Coffin' for their strange handling! They were briefly replaced by aircraft of No. 513 Flight, No. 241 Squadron of float seaplanes at Portland. Around Dorset, RNAS mooring stations for airships were planned for Upton, Toller (Bridport) and Moreton. Everything changed, and the local units disbanded, when the Royal Naval Air Service was absorbed into the new Royal Air Force on 1 April 1918.

EIGHT

SEEK AND STRIKE: SCIENCE AND SEA POWER

Despite the enormous losses at sea shipping was replaced at an impressive rate, especially after the United States became involved in the war. Even with their high strike rate the submarines could no longer bring the country to its knees by stopping movement at sea. The Germans had lost the war on land by the end of 1918, and on 11 November 1918 the Flag Officer Portland Command Area relayed a signal to all units of the Royal Navy under his command stating that 'hostilities will cease at 11:00 hours today'.

Just a week after the Armistice Dorset had a rare glimpse of American warships when the US Battleship Division 9, under Rear Admiral William S. Sims on USS *Wyoming*, stopped by at Portland. The battleships stayed for 2 weeks before sailing to rendezvous with President Woodrow Wilson on the USS *George Washington*, en route to the Paris Peace Conference.

Naval cadets continued to be trained at Portland after the war, and the former battleships HMS *Colossus* and HMS *Collingwood* were brought to the harbour for a few months in 1921 to augment the shore base.

Portland had many advantages over other south coast ports, but as it abutted the Island's steep hillside, it was hampered by the lack of flat land for shore-side development. To help overcome this, the 2000-ton capacity floating dock *AFD VII* was brought to the harbour in May 1914. It was removed for the duration of the war, but returned soon afterwards. Portland had a succession of floating docks through most of the twentieth century. In 1923 its huge dock – capable of holding

December 1918; the United States Battle Fleet assembled at Portland ready to sail to meet President Wilson at sea on his way to the Peace Conference. Among them were the big American 'Dreadnoughts' *New York, Oklahoma* and *Nevada*, under Admiral Rodgers.

H-Class submarines at Portland in 1920. Nine years later *H47* was sunk with the loss of twenty one of the crew after colliding with submarine *L12* off Milford Haven.

the biggest battleship – was towed 450 miles in 4 days by 6 Admiralty tugs.

The ending of hostilities enabled a more relaxed appraisal of the needs of the Navy in the area; there was even talk of closing the Portland base, or adapting it into a commercial port. However the sea off the Dorset coast was a naval training and exercise area without equal. It was particularly conducive to anti-submarine trials, which despite the peace-time cutbacks, continued at HMS *Sarepta*.

The cruiser HMS *Gibraltar* was brought to Portland to oversee the demobilisation of hundreds of anti-submarine trawlers which had almost filled the harbour between Weymouth and Portland. *Gibraltar* took over the anti-submarine role when HMS *Sarepta* closed temporarily in 1919.

Training squadrons or flotillas were based at Portland from 1919 down the years to 1981. The anti-submarine work expanded over the years to ultimately

The impressive-looking cruiser *Antrim* (1905) was re-commissioned for pioneering wireless asdic trials at Portland in 1920, and was the first ship to be fitted with an experimental sonar system. The base was already leading the world in anti-submarine detection.

Cab drivers like Fred Hoare, here at Castletown around 1920, carried sailors to the station for shore leave, or to the delights of Weymouth. Fred went on to found Bluebird Coaches of Dorset, still going strong 90 years later.

provide a full range of sea training and trials facilities.

The 1st Anti-submarine Flotilla comprised very shallow draft P- and PC-Boats which were berthed by the Coaling Pier. Crews of some of these patrol boats commented on their 'ability to roll on a damp flannel', but many left with fond and humorous memories. Second in command of P-31 was 18 year-old Sub Lieutenant Louis (later an Admiral of the Fleet and Lord) Mountbatten.

Anti-submarine technology was now advancing. The early trials of the experimental Type 112 ASDIC listening and detection sets in the P-Boats were so successful that training was stepped up, and the shore base HMS *Sarepta* reopened in 1920. The First Lord of the Admiralty enthused: 'The anti-submarine

This small Admiralty whaler *Icewhale* was renamed *Osprey* in 1924 to complement the newly reformed shore-based anti-submarine establishment, and the name was duly adopted for all the onshore research and training facilities. The name *Osprey* has been synonymous with maritime Portland ever since.

school has been set up in the existing buildings at Portland, and already there is considerable promise for the future in certain detection devices under trial.'

HMS *Gibraltar*, the parent ship to the 1st Anti-submarine Flotilla, was soon joined by four R-Class destroyers fitted with the latest type 115 ASDIC. However, the latter had a problem as its underwater steel dome crushed at speeds of over 20 knots. *Gibraltar* was relieved by HMS *Heather* in 1923, but the biggest change occurred on 1st April 1924 when *Sarepta*'s role was transferred to HMS *Osprey*. Its first captain, S.D. Tillard, initially based himself on a small Admiralty whaler called *Icewhale* (Z12) which was renamed *Osprey* to complement the shore base.

Britain's underwater research was consolidated three years later when Portsmouth's Anti-Submarine branch was absorbed into HMS *Osprey* at Portland. The setup was renamed the Anti-Submarine Experimental Establishment (A/SEE) in 1929.

Tripod and moored hydrophones had previously been laid on the seabed outside the Breakwater, and in 1923 the first submarine detecting loop was laid off the Shambles, the shallow shoal south-east of the Bill. Electrical signals were sent to special receivers in 'loop rooms' on shore.

Despite a new government veto on major naval and military building, the HMS *Osprey* research and training facilities expanded through the 1920s and 30s. In 1933 the Admiralty decided to fit all new destroyers and submarines with ASDIC. Ramshackle huts, affectionately known as 'Whipsnade', on the grassy undercliff slopes, were replaced in the late 1930s by a complex of large brick buildings.

Frederick 'Johnnie' Walker was an early trainee at HMS *Osprey*. 12 years later he returned to the base as its Experimental Commander, then as a commander in the Second World War. Walker sank more U-boats during the Battle of the Atlantic than any other British or Allied commander.

The striking crest of HMS *Osprey*, the bird of prey with a dogfish in its claws, has been familiar to the many thousands of men and women who have known this famous Dorset establishment in its various guises throughout the twentieth century. It was designed in 1923 by Cmdr HR Sawbridge, the school's commander. The Admiralty deliberated for six years before finally approving the design in 1929.

Although the challenges of war had brought rapid advances in submarine design and safety, it still took a special breed of sailor to venture below the waves. The sea off Dorset continued to claim victims.

On 10 January 1924 HM Submarine *L-24*, on a fleet exercise in Lyme Bay,

Proud symbolism. The bell and insignia of the Royal Naval Air Station, HMS *Osprey*.

HMS *Thruster* of the Dorset-based 1st Anti-Submarine Flotilla had a top speed of 33 knots. In 1928 she ran down and damaged submarine *R4* off Portland Bill, fortunately with no casualties, and later took part in the search for *M2* using her sonar.

was rammed by the 29,000-ton battleship HMS *Resolution*. *Resolution* was rising and dipping in a swell, and came down on the ascending submarine. The sub sank instantly with the loss of her entire crew of 43. She lies at 52 metres down, and the angle of her hydroplanes indicate that she was trying to make a hard dive to avoid the collision.

HM Submarine *M2* left Portland at 9 am on the 26th January 1932 to take part in routine exercises. At 10:11 she radioed her intention to dive at 10:30. No more was heard. The alarm was raised only when *M2* failed to return to port in late afternoon. Search vessels raced to West Bay but there was no sign of the submarine or her

A revolutionary – but ultimately disastrous – innovation was the conversion of the submarine HMS *M2* as the World's first submersible aircraft carrier, complete with a hangar and catapults launch to launch a tiny folding-wing seaplane. In January 1932 the vessel failed to surface in Lyme Bay, entombing her crew of 60.

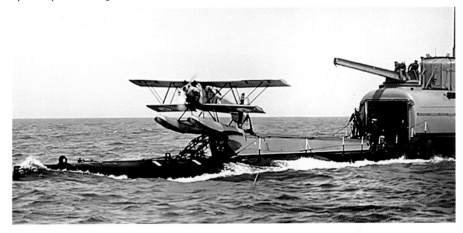

Keeping in step was never easy down the steep New Road on Portland. An appeal for 'HM Submarines' (probably after the *M2* disaster 1932) is on the wall poster, right.

crew. The captain of the coaster *Tynesider* reported seeing a submarine diving stern first off Portland, but it was a week before the submarine was located by the destroyer *Torrid* using ASDIC [sonar]. She lay on the seabed with her stern in the silt. The *M2* was a 1600-ton submarine of a revolutionary design built for the Royal Navy in 1918. She initially carried an enormous 12 inch gun, but this was removed after the Washington Naval Treaty of 1928 prohibited weapons of that calibre on submarines. In its place a hangar and catapult launch were installed for a folding-wing seaplane, a tiny Parnall Peto, making the *M2* the world's first submarine aircraft carrier. It appears that the submarine had commenced diving before the hangar doors were fully closed. Two bodies were recovered from the wreck during the next week, but the rest of her crew of 60 remain entombed. Arduous salvage attempts went on for months before being abandoned.

The war left the country in a financial straitjacket. Military and naval forces were severely cut back, but most core facilities at Portland were maintained. Even in peace Dorset's naval base had become indispensable to the Admiralty. By the early 1920s Portland was an important rendezvous for the Atlantic Fleet, which spent the majority of its time here on exercises. The port had excellent coaling facilities, and the number of oil fuel storage tanks was increased. It was the base for the Anti-Submarine Flotilla and the 1st Minesweeping Flotilla, while in the port cadet training was undertaken on HMS *Colossus*, HMS *Orion* and various submarines. HMS *Fermoy* was the home of the Periscope School. *Fermoy* served in both world wars but was destroyed after being bombed in the Mediterranean in 1941.

The port had always been a naval base in all but name, but was not until 1923 that it was formally designated as *HM Naval Base, Portland*.

NINE

THE NAVY PREPARES

Throughout the 1920s and 1930s the Dorset coast frequently resounded to the sound of gunnery practice. Two of the Royal Navy's principal gunnery practice ships at Portland were veterans of the Battle of Jutland; the battle-cruiser HMS *Tiger* from 1924, and *Iron Duke* which relieved her in 1929. When HMS *Hood* – the largest warship in the world – fired salvos, the boom of her guns could be felt in towns and villages all over the county.

The 44,600-tons HMS *Hood,* later to become one of the Royal Navy's most famous and tragic vessels, came to Dorset soon after her launch in early 1920, the first of many visits to the area. While at Portland later that year, she supplied Marines to form a guard of honour for the internment of the Unknown Warrior at Westminster Abbey.

Hood's log of June 1922 records that she departed from Weymouth for Swanage Bay to conduct submarine attack exercises. On her way back she practiced her 15-inch guns. Next January *Hood* carried out 'action stations' and 'inclination' exercises with HMS *Resolution* off Portland, before leaving with the Atlantic Fleet for Gibraltar. In May that year she was recommissioned as the flagship of the Cruiser Squadron, Atlantic Fleet, and the next month she was off to Bournemouth for a courtesy trip. In port between exercises, like many capacious ships, *Hood*

Sport was always essential for a fit Navy. This was a match between HM Minesweepers and HMS *Coventry* in the 1930s, played on fine recreation grounds laid out near Castletown in 1905-7. The fields survived the departure of the Royal Navy from the area, only to be built over in 2011.

The heavy 15' guns of the great battle cruiser HMS *Hood* during manoeuvres off Dorset in 1926. HMS *Repulse* is following.

often hosted concert parties. Ashore, the towns livened up when descended upon by thousands of officers and men from the fleets.

The sheer size and power of HMS *Hood* made her stand out every time she came to Dorset. Crew member Fred White recalled: 'One felt secure in South Dorset, as the *Hood's* guns spoke for Britain, and to see the foretop of her above the Hotels on Weymouth Front from the hills inland as she lay at anchor in Weymouth Bay . . . thousands of holiday-makers who lined Weymouth Pier watched thousands of bluejackets pour ashore. It was a delight to watch the boat hook drill and to note picket boats from the *Hood, Repulse, Renown* and the battleships. And in the darkness, the sky being criss-crossed by dozens of searchlights.'

Searchlight displays in Weymouth Bay and Portland Harbour were truly impressive. Shafts of light darting at crazy angles across the sky, brightly illuminating the underside of any passing cloud, was a sight never to be forgotten.

The Royal Navy has always relished the chance to demonstrate its sea power. The pride of Britain's Senior Service was seen at its best at the many Royal Naval Reviews, especially in the first half of the twentieth century. Most reviews were at Spithead, but Weymouth and Portland also experienced several spectaculars.

HMS *Courageous* hosted King George V for his review the fleet on 12 July, 1932. With him were the Prince of Wales and Prince George who took a 28 minute

Powerful carbon-arc searchlights fitted to naval vessels were vital components of anti-aircraft strategy before the development of acoustic and radar devices. The Royal Navy impressed the public with spectacular searchlight displays, as here in July 1932.

flight in a Fairey IIIF reconnaissance plane for 'air experience'. *Courageous* had been laid down in 1915, and in 1928 became one of the first ships to be rebuilt as a proper aircraft carrier.

By 1936 tensions with Germany were rising rapidly, and the government decided to embark on a major rearmament scheme. Investment in naval hardware had been at rock bottom in the 1920s and early 1930s. However even by 1939 only one completely new aircraft carrier had been built; HMS Ark Royal.

Fierce weather greeted the arrival in Dorset of the uncrowned King Edward VIII in November 1936 to inspect the newly rebuilt establishment HMS *Osprey*. On the arrival of the Royal train at Portland the sea, whipped up by a raging gale broke over Chesil Beach and flooded the station. His Majesty was towed into a siding in his carriage with floodwater up to its axles, and he slept through it all! The following morning, the King's car ploughed through the water, cheered onto the naval base by raincoated crowds. The guns of the Home Fleet's flagship HMS *Nelson* boomed their salute.

Things did not go too well when he arrived at HMS *Osprey*. Guiding the royal party around the laboratory was an aging gunner who happened to be stone deaf. The King did not appear amused when his repeated questions went unanswered, and he called for his car without inspecting the staff or seeing the elaborate equipment laid out for his inspection. The king clearly had other priorities. He had expressed the wish to hear a ship's concert, so for days auditions had been held on the carrier HMS *Courageous* in Weymouth Bay. Once aboard in the carrier's 2000 seat hangar and by now totally at ease, he brought the house down by playing

The battleship HMS *Nelson* firing her powerful 16' guns off Dorset. Commissioned in 1930, *Nelson* was the flagship of the Home Fleet and saw action throughout the Second World War.

the bones in a stokers' mouth organ band. This turned out to be one of his last engagements as monarch, for within a month he had announced his abdication.

Submarines obviously had extremely restricted space for stores and supplies so had to be serviced from their depot ships at frequent intervals. Successive depot ships were stationed in the harbour to 'mother' the reserve and active submarines. HMS *Lucia* was originally a German civilian liner which was captured in 1914 and converted to a submarine depot ship. *Vulcan*, converted from an 1889 torpedo boat carrier, was on station until being relieved by HMS *Titania* in 1930.

Meanwhile training and secret anti-submarine and detection research continued apace at HMS *Osprey*. In 1938 Winston Churchill and the First Sea Lord, Admiral Dudley Pound, came to see for themselves the latest ASDIC and sonar developments.

They were quickly followed by HM King George VI, his brother the Duke of Kent and Lord Louis Mountbatten, who came for the 1938 Royal Review of the Home Fleet. From the flagship *Nelson* in Weymouth Bay they watched colourful and impressive fleet manoeuvres, 'demonstrating Britain's Rule of the Waves'. No doubt the king also reflected on his days as a young midshipman at Portland.

They peered through binoculars to see guns scoring a direct hit on a radio-controlled Queen Bee pilotless plane, sending it crashing into the sea. In the following June there were six Queen Bee aircraft at Portland. They flew at about 70 mph at 5000 feet and although on a straight course some survived four days of intensive shooting.

The king came back on 9 August 1939 on probably the last excursion of the

In the mid-1930s the battleships *Nelson* and *Rodney* (pictured) practiced anti-aircraft gunnery in Weymouth Bay, against a remote-controlled 'Queen Bee' target plane.

elegant Royal Yacht *Victoria & Albert III* before she was laid up. More ominously, war was just 3 weeks away, and of the ships proudly assembled nearly half were to be lost in the coming conflict. For two hours the royal barge beat against a strong north-easterly wind between the long lines of ships in Weymouth Bay. Leading the fleet was the ill-fated aircraft carrier *Courageous*, the flagship of Vice Admiral Sir Max Horton. At dusk thousands of 'fairy lights' were switched on, drawing a scintillating profile of each of the 130 ships stretching across the bay.

Maritime Dorset's descent into war in the late 1930s is well described by Captain W.R. Fell. He was in command of a group of H-class reserve submarines attached to the 'ancient little depot ship' *Alecto* at Portland. His flotillas were involved in supporting the active submarines, in training, depth charge and target practice.

'Attack on a heavily screened fleet with air cover was as near the real thing as any peacetime exercise could be. It was exciting beyond dreams. The fleet was on its toes, knowing submarines to be in the vicinity. Everyone was against you personally, to catch you by ASDICs, to drop a charge and put you out of the attack, to baffle you by sharp, irregular alterations of course and speed. Every lookout's eye was skinned for the sight of a cautiously raised periscope; but to worm your way in past cruisers and destroyers, then fire your fish at the flagship and hit with two of the salvo – that indeed was triumph.'

When his squadron broke off on a tour around the country, Fell and his crews 'had such a wonderful round of parties and entertainments that the return to work at Portland seemed very dull.' As tension rose in 1938 and into 1939, the training increased steadily in volume and intensity as more ships came to Portland for anti-submarine training.

'As the last few weeks of peace were used up, Portland woke from its long sleep

Battleship HMS *Nelson* (top left) and submarine depot ship HMS *Titania* (right) at Portland in 1933. The Aberdare/Hunt class minesweepers at the jetty were to play a crucial part in keeping vital sea lanes open throughout the Second World War.

H-class submarines under the command of Captain W.R. Fell, were attached to the 'ancient little depot ship' *Alecto* at Portland. In the late 1930s this reserve flotilla was involved in supporting the active submarines in training, depth charge and target practice.

and became a seething hive of ships and activity. All five of my H-boats were fully manned, and CEOs were busy storing, running trials and working up when the warning signal "Prepare for War" came, sending cold shivers down many spines.'

All torpedo practice heads were now replaced by live warheads. Secret envelopes were opened and their contents studied, codes and ciphers changed and everyone worked day and night. When exercising his *H31* in West Bay, Captain Fell surfaced in darkness, and through heavy fog, saw a light which was assumed to be a marauding U-boat. He could even see phosphorescent ripples from its bow. He pursued it – and promptly grounded on the shingle off Bridport. He had been attacking a generating station ½ mile inland!

'Then suddenly Portland was empty. We woke one morning to find the harbour cleared. *Titania* and her flotilla had left for their war station at Blyth. All the frigates, corvettes, sloops and destroyers had vanished and only *Alecto* and her H-boats and a few harbour craft remained. There was an uncanny hush before the storm broke over us that was to sweep all we had known before it.'

Captain Fell recalled: 'The morning of 3rd September (1939) broke clear, calm and hot. We moved restlessly about, expecting we knew not what, but thinking all the time about what we remembered of War I, its courage and fury . . .'

At 11 a.m. they gathered around the wireless in the wardroom, heard Big Ben chime and then Mr Chamberlain's solemn voice telling them they were at war. 'A signal man waited, listening at the door, then came to me with a message: "*H31*-proceed with all dispatch to rendezvous with *Kelly* 4 miles 260˚ from Portland Bill and carry out A.S.P.6". The war had come for me.'

HMS *Kelly* had been completed just 10 days before, and came straight to Portland to work-up prior to taking up war station. In command of her and of the entire 5th Destroyer Flotilla was Captain Lord Louis Mountbatten. Action came soon. On day two of the war *Kelly* and HM Destroyer *Acheron* detected a supposed U-Boat off Portland, and duly deployed a depth charge. Eighty feet below a huge explosion rocked Captain Fell's *H31* with 'an almighty crash and flash, lights went out and shattered, men fell sprawling . . .' Mountbatten had nearly made the first submarine 'kill' of the war, but not one he would have been proud of! *H31* shot up and raced well clear before Kelly returned and dropped four more depth charges.

On 17th September *Kelly* rushed to the Western approaches to take on survivors from the *Courageous*, sunk that day by U-boat *U29* with the loss of 519 lives. After completing her work-up at Portland, *Kelly* was deployed to the Mediterranean, where off Crete on 23 May 1941 she too was attacked and sunk. Mountbatten was one of 38 survivors, but 128 men died. A year later Mountbatten's exploits in the doomed *Kelly* inspired the great patriotic war film *In Which We Serve*, directed by David Lean and starring Noël Coward. Appropriately, the Ministry of Information cleared security for location shots to be filmed at Portland.

TEN

THE SECOND WORLD WAR

Early in the war Dorset found itself in an extremely vulnerable position, far more so than in the First World War. The fall of France in 1940 brought its coast within a 20 minutes flight range for the Luftwaffe. The Navy lost no time in deploying discreet defences at all potential invasion points, especially the harbours at Poole, Weymouth and Portland.

Large fleets in Portland harbour could no longer be adequately defended, and the Royal Navy's main warships were desperately needed at other fronts. The H-class submarines departed in early May 1940, and most other naval ships followed in a move vindicated by the German air raids which followed. During the long hot summer that history now calls the Battle of Britain, Portland/Weymouth was the target of more formation aerial raids than anywhere else in the country after London and Liverpool.

On the outbreak of war HMS *Foylebank* was converted from a civilian freighter to an anti-aircraft ship. Through June 1940 she was defending Channel convoys, and mooring overnight in Portland Harbour. On 4 July *Foylebank*'s own radar picked up aircraft approaching. Being still at her moorings she was a stationary target, when at 8:40 am a wave of 33 bombers appeared out of the sun from the east. After sweeping around Verne Hill they paired off to dive bomb the ship. Her guns blazed defiantly but she was overwhelmed by the ferocious attack. A pall of smoke rose high into the clear sky as she was engulfed in fire. This was the

The Royal Naval Cemetery occupies a tranquil setting overlooking Portland Harbour. It was laid out in the 19th century and is the final resting place of sailors from various nations. The headstone in the foreground marks the grave of Jack Mantle, who was awarded a posthumous Victoria Cross for his role in the attack on the *Foylebank*.

Luftwaffe's first major attack on Dorset during the Second World War. It lasted just 8 minutes but survivor Frank Pavey said 'It was like a nightmare and seemed to go on forever'. Pavey was working the ammo hoist on the starboard pom-pom when the first bomb cut all the electrics. 'The well deck and pom-pom 'band stand' looked like a butcher's shop – bits and pieces of body everywhere. I don't know how I got away with it. All I had was a nick across my shin.'

23-year-old Leading Seaman Jack Mantle remained at his damaged gun, switched to manual operation and continued firing at the diving planes. His gun crew were dead or dying, his leg was badly mangled and then he got hit in the chest, but he kept firing to the last. There were numerous acts of bravery that day, but for his tenacity Jack was awarded a posthumous Victoria Cross, the only one to be won by the Navy in British home waters. This young hero's name lives forever in the annals of Dorset's maritime history.

Several other vessels were sunk that sunny morning, but out of *Foylebank*'s crew of 19 officers and 279 crew, 176 men were killed.

Warships were frequently attacked off Dorset by the Luftwaffe. Near St Albans Head on 11 July 1940 Junkers 87 dive bombers destroyed the submarine escort *Warrior II*, an aging and lightly armed converted luxury yacht. Nine days later destroyer HMS *Beagle* survived an attack off Portland Bill, but HMS *Delight* was not so lucky: 20 miles south of Portland she caught fire after a dive bomb attack and had to be abandoned.

In the autumn of 1940 three Portland based patrol trawlers were mined. Six men on HMS *Loch Monteith* were killed when she was damaged by a mine 10 miles south of Portland Bill. HMS *Recoil*, a captured German trawler exploded and vanished without trace, and on 22 October the 6-months old *Hickory* was sunk with the loss of 20 men.

Intense raids continued by day and by night, and several merchant ships were mined off the Shambles; in August its lightship was towed into harbour for the duration of the war. Portland lighthouse and all shore lights were extinguished as soon as the local Observer Corps identified hostile aircraft approaching. Blockships were prepared to blockade Weymouth and Poole Harbours, and loaded torpedo tubes were installed on the Portland Breakwater heads to cover the ship channels.

The shore establishment HMS *Osprey* was cleared in late 1940 and the whole training and anti-submarine operation was transferred to Scotland. In the vacated buildings a new coastal forces base, HMS *Attack*, was commissioned in January 1941. Under a new 'Flag Officer Coastal Forces', its remit was to build up flotillas of motor torpedo boats, motor gunboats and motor launches, so that attacks could be launched on the enemy-held French coast.

In September 1942 what was described as the 'Stone Frigate', HMS *Bee*, was established in guest houses and various other buildings close to Weymouth Harbour. Working-up involved morning lectures in the Alexandra Gardens Theatre which also doubled as a canteen, and torpedo and gunnery firing exercises in the

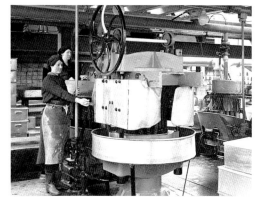

Women munition workers preparing the mix for cordite production at the Royal Naval Cordite Factory on Holton Heath. Operating in utmost secrecy, work at the factory was extremely hazardous. At the peak of the war, it employed nearly 4,000 people. Today its site is occupied by the Holton Heath Business Park.

bay. Within six months 17 boats from *Bee* were undertaking full-scale Coastal Forces Exercises with realistic night attacks.

Degaussing (DG) ranges were installed outside the harbour to counter the magnetic mines which the Germans were now deploying. The young prisoners at the Borstal Institution on Portland were put at the disposal of the Navy to make the huge coils for demagnetising ships, some of which comprised 30 miles of cable.

The nature of hostilities off Dorset was changing, and from mid 1942 the main actions involved German E-boat attacks on convoys. The merchant vessels were escorted by various naval ships including trawlers and Hunt-Class destroyers.

Work was stepped up at the Whitehead's Torpedo Works at Wyke Regis, where some 1500 people were now employed. The factory was obviously a prime target and it was bombed on the 1st May 1941. Despite heavy damage torpedo production continued unabated.

Cordite manufacture at the RN Holton Heath site continued through the war, despite being hit by 10 enemy bombs. Two decoy sites were built, one on Brownsea Island, the second near the village of Arne, where during night raids

Poole Harbour's Defence Motor Launch. These armed and highly manoeuvrable HDMLs were built in local shipyards, and proved invaluable in combat and mine-laying roles.

fires and pyrotechnics were lit to simulate bomb explosions, to fool the German bombers into believing they had hit the factory.

All Dorset coastal towns were now heavily involved in the naval war effort. The naval dockyard at Portland was extremely busy. The yard was involved in adaptation of the Royal Naval Auxiliary Hospital at Sherborne, and on a temporary Royal Naval Hospital at Minterne House, once the home of Admiral Robert Digby, a captain at Trafalgar.

Following the defeat of the Low Countries in 1940, the Navy escorted vessels bringing Dutch and Belgian naval and military personnel and their families to the safe seclusion of Brownsea Island, now designated a Reception and Quarantine Centre. In the first week 600 men, women and children were uncomfortably housed in tents and huts, and over six weeks more than 3000 refugees were 'processed' on the island before being dispersed around the country.

In 1940 the Fleet Air Arm acquired the premises of the Royal Motor Yacht Club in Poole Harbour and other sites for Royal Naval Air Station (RNAS) Sandbanks; officially HMS *Daedalus II* but also called HMS *Tadpole*. Based there were Royal Naval Air Squadrons 765 and 766 with their 18 seaplanes. The Sandbanks Yacht Co. was also taken over and its boatshed was cleared for seaplanes storage. One luxury yacht belonging to the band leader Billy Cotton was retained for hospitality purposes.

A vacated RAF site at Hamworthy was commissioned as amphibious training base HMS *Turtle* in October 1942. It was a combined operations centre for some 4000 American and Canadian and British troops arriving for training and beach exercises, in preparation for the D-Day landings. In Poole the 3rd Special Services Brigade was formed from No.5 Commando, joined by No.1 Commando and Nos. 42 and 44 Royal Marines. The wide expanse of Poole Harbour was ideal for assault training, and night landing exercises were carried out on Brownsea Island and at Shell Bay.

Meanwhile Portland dockyard personnel started preparing for the great attack on German-held France. They built three slips for LCTs ('Landing Craft, Tanks') at the Dorset Yacht Company at Poole and two at Castletown. All Dorset boatyards were turned over to war production, and Bolson and Co. of Poole was one of several non-boatbuilding firms who responded to an appeal to make landing craft. In a short time they were producing one every day.

The dockyard also installed equipment and slipways for LCM ('Landing Craft, Mechanical' for carrying vehicles) at Ridge, near Wareham, and at the Backwater (Inner Harbour) at Weymouth where in the absence of a suitable slip, a special 30 ton crane had to be imported from America.

Admiralty floating dock *No.7* proved invaluable for the repair of damaged ships at Portland, although it had previously been hit by a bomb while it had HMT *Hertfordshire* lifted dry. The ship and the dock were saved by the efforts of the mechanical staff, for which two men were awarded the British Empire Medal.

A Fairey Seafox coming ashore at RNAS *Sandbanks* (formally HMS *Daedalus* II) in 1942. The Poole Harbour base was established in 1940 for the training of aircrew of 764 & 765 Naval Air Squadrons, which also flew Supermarine Walrus and Fairy Swordfish aircraft.

As preparations for D-Day gathered pace, the physical work around Dorset's coastal towns intensified. The functions of HMS *Bee* were transferred to Liverpool, and the Weymouth sites were then used as a combined operational base; HMS *Grasshopper*.

In February 1943 the coastal force craft MTB 344 left Portland with Commandos on a lone and hazardous visit to the occupied Channel Islands to destroy a semaphore station. HMS *Tadpole* was disbanded in October 1943 to make way for D-Day preparations.

The following February, King George VI, Winston Churchill and Generals Eisenhower and Montgomery, arrived by Royal Train at Swanage to watch Allied forces practicing amphibious operations at Studland Bay. Clandestine operations were stepped up. By April 1944 British shore radar could detect German boats as far away as Cherbourg harbour.

Beach landing exercises on a huge scale were carried out at Poole, Studland and Weymouth, and at Slapton Sands, Devon. In Exercise *Tiger* on the evening of 27 April 1944 a convoy of 8 Landing Ship Tanks (LSTs) with 4000 men aboard headed across Lyme Bay for landing practice at Slapton. After midnight and out of the darkness, nine fast German torpedo boats suddenly appeared. Three LSTs were torpedoed, two sank and one was severely damaged, resulting in the death of 749 U.S. men; four times more than were lost by Force U in its D-Day landing in France. Hundreds of bodies were washed up on Chesil Beach and taken to Castletown Pier, Portland. The whole tragic episode was kept in utmost secrecy to avoid alerting the enemy to the strategy. Even 60 years later there were lingering accusations of an official 'cover-up', especially regarding the disposal of the bodies. This was the most costly training incident for U.S. forces during the entire Second World War.

The idea of constructing floating Mulberry Harbours to be conveyed to the French coast was conceived in 1943. Some of the enormous Phoenix sections

The US Navy assembles at Castletown. The preparation for D-Day embarkations from the Dorset ports demanded logistical planning on a colossal scale.

were tested on the east side of Weymouth Bay and strung together by the Royal Navy. As D-Day approached, eighty-five US and British tugboats were readied to tow 150 gigantic floating blocks across the Channel to form the huge breakwaters. Despite the total destruction of the American segment by a storm, for the rest of the year and into 1945, the Mulberry Harbour successfully sheltered hundreds of vessels of all sizes, and made a huge contribution to the success of the Allied assault.

On 1 May 1944 Portland-Weymouth was formally commissioned as the United States Navy Advanced Amphibious Base (USNAAB). Tight security greeted the King when he arrived at the base on 25 May, along with Winston Churchill and the Free French Leader General De Gaulle, to see the preparations for themselves.

By 5 June there was a huge concentration of shipping across Weymouth Bay and Portland harbour. Thousands of U.S. troops boarded landing craft at Weymouth, and tanks and vehicles were loaded at Portland. Under flagship USS *Ancon* were 13 assault ships, 15 U.S. and British destroyers, the 31st Minesweeper Flotilla of the Royal Canadian Navy, and the RN's 4th Minesweeping Flotilla which had laid buoys marking the swept lanes out into the Channel. Ready also were five steam gunboats, plus the numerous landing craft, moored in lines across Portland harbour.

Everything was ready to go by June 5, loading was completed for the first phase of Operation Neptune, but heavy weather caused a 24-hour postponement. Force

A torpedo boat of the Support Squadron from HMS *Turtle* based at Hamworthy and US coast-guard cutters of Rescue Flotilla I alongside Poole Quay.

Gunboats returning to Poole after dawn from an anti E-boat patrol off Cherbourg (IWM A 24047).

'U' had already sailed from Devon but the gale forced them back to Weymouth Bay which became even more congested. Then, by midnight on 5 June the whole area had virtually emptied of ships. Throughout the night there was a continuous drone of troop carrying planes and towed gliders flying over Dorset to Normandy. Off St Albans Head the British cruiser *Glasgow* rendezvoused with U.S. battleships *Texas* and *Arkansas*, two Free French cruisers, and several U.S. and British destroyers from Portland. Under cover of darkness they joined the mighty Force 'O' and headed for 'Omaha' Beach.

As for the action on the French shores 'the rest is history', but German mines and E-boats still caused casualties to Allied warships and supply ships in the Channel. On the morning of 13 June the destroyer HMS *Boadicea* was hit by a torpedo dropped from a Junkers 88. She exploded and sank within minutes 16 miles south-west of Portland, and there were only 12 survivors.

When victory in France had been secured, a U.S. Army message to Portland and Weymouth said: 'You are the biggest little port in the world, you have been

73

HMS *Boadicea* sank in three minutes after being torpedoed by a Junkers 88 off Portland on 13 June 1944 with the loss of 178 men, despite Luftwaffe attacks being curbed after D-Day.

wonderful.' Commemoration stones were unveiled at Weymouth and Portland to mark the area's major contribution to the conquest of the French coast.

Poole was the third largest embarkation point for D-Day landings of Operation Overlord. 81 landing craft left Poole Harbour for Omaha Beach with American troops from the 29th Infantry Division and the US Army Rangers. The port afterwards served as a base for supplies to the allied forces in Europe.

As the war was brought to a conclusion several surrendered German submarines were brought to Dorset. On 4 May 1945 the Admiralty directed the German High Command to order U-boats to proceed to specified ports. The *U-249* was the first German submarine to surrender at the end of the war on 9 May 1945, escorted into Weymouth by the frigates *Amethyst* and *Magpie*. The White Ensign was raised on her conning tower, and she was then moved to Portland. A succession of surrendering U-boats followed and all were taken to Castletown for examination.

Surrendered German submarines U-1023 and U-249 tied up at Portland on 10 May 1945. The crews were taken to a prisoner of war transit camp at the nearby naval officers sports field.

ELEVEN

A WATCHFUL PEACE

After the last beach landings in France in April 1945, the landing craft organization was disbanded. The Royal Navy's part in the war from Dorset had been conducted by three Flag Officers-in-Charge of the Portland Sub-Command: Vice-Admiral E. R. Drummond; Vice-Admiral G. T. C. P. Swabey; and Rear-Admiral R. J. R. Scott. The Flag Officer's flag was finally hauled down in July 1945.

As hostilities ended Dorset was faced with years of recovery. 10,000 naval and military personnel left Portland-Weymouth, and thousands more dispersed from the east of the county. The ports, harbours and boatyards reverted to peacetime roles, but new threats were emerging and despite being virtually broke, the country felt the need to maintain a strong Navy.

HMS *Osprey* returned from Scotland in 1946. In the following year it was commissioned as HM Underwater Detection Establishment (UDE), for scientific and communications research. The anti-submarine flotilla also returned to its original base in Portland. This comprised the destroyers *Escapade* and *Eggesford*, frigate *Helmsdale*, and corvettes *Tintagel Castle*, *Leeds Castle* and *Oxford Castle*.

The Phoenix units of the Mulberry Harbour were put to good use after the war. Ten of the 7,700 ton units were towed to Portland in 1946 to provide shelter for

After an active war service with the British Home and Pacific fleets, the battleship HMS *Howe* spent four years at Portland as flagship of the Training Squadron. By then, battleships had become an expensive and increasingly obsolete form of naval hardware.

The Phoenix units which made up the enormous Mulberry Harbour played a critical part in the success of the D-Day landings. These segments were brought to Portland after the war to provide shelter for the construction works of the new Queens Pier.

the site of a new long pier within the harbour. This was the Queens or 'Q' Pier which greatly extended the port's berthing capacity, including latest Battle-class destroyers. It was completed in the early 1950s. Two remaining sections which for years had lain on the seabed near Portland Breakwater were raised in 1963 and positioned again as gigantic permanent windbreaks for Q Pier.

Battleships, destroyers and Castle-class frigates resumed their traditional Spring

1946. Pioneer Alan Bristow lands his primitive Sikorsky R4B Hoverfly onto the deck of the frigate HMS *Helmsdale* in Portland Harbour. It was the first ever helicopter landing on an escort vessel.

Here the Home Fleet is assembled at Portland in May 1952 ready for the summer exercises. HMS *Vanguard*, flagship of Admiral Creasy, was the Navy's biggest, most powerful and last ever battleship. However, the future lay with aircraft carriers like HMS *Indomitable* beyond.

Cruises from Portland, albeit with many fewer ships than before the war. The Royal Naval Training Squadron (the 'Portland Squadron') was established in 1948. That year the crews and destroyers of the Third Escort Flotilla were extras in the film 'Morning Departure', starring Richard Attenborough and John Mills. Filmed partly off Portland and Weymouth it was about the ordeals of a submarine that failed to surface after trials; so it was close to home for those who had witnessed such disasters for real.

Just as aeroplanes arrived at Portland within nine years of the first powered flight, so in 1946 helicopters were based there only four years after the first production one took to the air. The task of testing the revolutionary Sikorsky R-4B Hoverfly for the Navy was given to HMS *Osprey*, utilising the old First World War seaplane slipway at the Naval Base. The R.N. helicopter operations were then moved to Lee-on-Solent, but not before Lt. Alan Bristow made the first landing of a helicopter on a Royal Naval ship, the frigate HMS *Helmsdale*. Lt. K Reed made another pioneering landing off Portland on 1st February 1947 onto the deck of HMS *Vanguard* as she departed with the King and Queen and the two princesses for the Royal Tour of South Africa.

HMS *Vanguard* was the Navy's biggest, most powerful and last ever battleship, and was the ninth vessel of that name. The length of the first *Vanguard*, which fought against the Spanish Armada, exactly equalled the battleship *Vanguard*'s width, 180 feet (55m). After her 1944 launch by Princess Elizabeth, *Vanguard* was frequently in Dorset waters. She was based at Portland from 1949 to 1951 heading

The Royal Navy's worst post-war peacetime disaster occurred in October 1948. A pinnace liberty boat carrying crew back to HMS *Illustrious* after a night out in Weymouth sank in stormy water just inside the Breakwater. Twenty-nine young men drowned.

the Training Squadron, flying the flag of C-in-C Home Fleet for the seasonal cruises. Its crew of 1500 officers and men included midshipmen from Canada and India and many trainees doing National Service. To feed them the ship's bakery made half a ton of bread a day, and young seamen on average gained a stone in weight during their 18 weeks training! The huge battleship carried 8 x 15-inch guns, 16 x 5.25-inch guns and 70 small AA guns. Its engines developed 130,000 hp and an engineer's tour of inspection involved a journey of 7 miles and ascending and descending 3000 feet.

In the Home Fleet manoeuvres of 1948 Lord Hall, the First Lord of the Admiralty, and Admiral Sir Rhoderick McGregor sailed in HMS *Duke of York* accompanied by destroyers and motor torpedo boats and two aircraft carriers. The *Duke of York* left Portland in February 1949, destined for the Arctic with a mixed fleet and aircraft including Sea Furys (802 Squadron), Fireflies (814 Squadron), Barracudas, Vampires, Firebrands, Sea Otters, and 9 Firefly helicopters. 'Operation Rusty' was to study the effects of very cold weather conditions on naval personnel and materials.

Regrettably tragedies did not end with the war. In 1948 the aircraft carrier HMS *Illustrious* was at Portland. Among her crew were trainees doing National Service. On 17 October many of the young men enjoyed a break ashore at Weymouth. On their late evening return in the ship's pinnaces the sea was already whipped up by a squall rising to gale force. After passing through the Breakwater entrance one started shipping water. Those aboard tried desperately to bail out with everything they could lay their hands on, but it was to no avail and the pinnace sank with the loss of 29 men. The 18-year-old midshipman who was in charge of the boat

HMS *Maidstone* was the large 'mother' ship for the 2nd and 7th Submarine Flotillas. She was moored almost permanently in Portland from 1946 until becoming a C-in-C Home Fleet's flagship in 1956. She departed when Portland ceased to be a submarine base two years later.

and drowned was blamed for the disaster, a verdict which many deemed totally unfair. In a moving ceremony in October 2010, the First Sea Lord, Admiral Sir Mark Stanhope, unveiled a stone memorial to the tragedy at Portland Marina.

HMS *Zodiac* was one of many vessels to serve through the early 1950s in the Portland Flotilla, which had the job of 'ping-running' with ASDIC classes from HMS *Osprey. Zodiac* was also involved in trials for the first ever directional sonobuoys and for the U.K.'s first underwater telephone. The Castle-class frigates of the Portland Squadron were replaced in 1956 with Type 14 frigates which formed the backbone of the squadron for the next 15 years. HMS *Undaunted* was brought in for trials and floating sonar tests, and by 1958 the squadron comprised eight frigates, two experimental ships, anti-submarine trawlers, a minesweeper and a mine location vessel.

At 8:30 am on 16 June 1955 the author, on a school bus on the Portland-Weymouth causeway, looked across the harbour to see a huge plume of smoke billowing skyward from the south-east corner of the harbour. This was the moment that an explosion ripped through the submarine *Sidon* and instantly killed 12 of the crew. It was caused by the premature detonation of volatile high test hydrogen peroxide propellant in a torpedo tube. HMS *Sidon* was an S-Class submarine with the Portland Training Squadron. Several S-, T- and U-class boats were lying alongside the Depot Ship *Maidstone*, and on hearing the alarm signal the destroyer HMS *Tyrian* raced to her with divers aboard. 43 men managed to escape, and Lt Charles Rhodes (27), a temporary surgeon on the *Maidstone*, dashed onto the sinking sub and pulled out five men. Tragically he was suffocated while trying to rescue the sixth, and for his bravery was posthumously awarded

HMS *Sidon*. A memorial to the 13 men who died when hydrogen peroxide propellant detonated prematurely was unveiled on the 50th anniversary of the tragedy at Portland Heights, overlooking the harbour.

In March 1958 the atomic powered USS *Skate* surfaced off Portland and slid into the harbour after making a record-breaking crossing of the Atlantic in 8 days 11 hours, submerged all the way.

the Albert Medal.

Submarine technology was advancing rapidly, and since 1951 the Admiralty had been preparing to move towards nuclear propulsion. The Royal Navy was working closely with the US Navy, and it was arranged for the new USS *Nautilus* to visit Portland in October 1957. Defence Minister Mr Duncan Sandys and the First Sea Lord, Lord Louis Mountbatten, greeted her, and defence contractors and designers were able to inspect the world's first nuclear powered submarine at close quarters.

Just five months later a second nuclear submarine, USS *Skate*, surfaced off Portland and slid into the harbour after making a record-breaking crossing of the Atlantic in 8 days 11 hours, submerged all the way. This was significant as the Royal Navy's first atomic submarine, the *Dreadnought*, was to follow closely the design of the *Skate*.

In August 1958 the *Nautilus* made a truly historic voyage from Pearl Harbor, Honolulu, on a perilous voyage which took her under the ice at the North Pole. Her first port of call again was Portland, England, where the world's press and news-film cameramen were there to record the occasion. It was a proud day for Dorset.

Nuclear armament brought heightened fears in the Cold War, and the Navy

Sailors of the aircraft carrier HMS *Indefatigable* ready to land at Weymouth for time ashore. The MFV following is from HMS *Vanguard*.

regarded underwater warfare as one of the main threats to all forms of shipping. The Admiralty thus embarked on a huge expansion of the work carried out by HMS *Osprey*. All the specialist underwater research and development units scattered around the country were consolidated at Portland. Through nearly half a century of amalgamations and reorganisations, the business went through several name changes, finally ending up as the Admiralty Research Establishment (ARE). Various branches were established around Dorset but the hub was two huge complexes which the Admiralty built between 1949 and 1952 at Southwell, and at East Weares, Portland. Attached to the Establishment were always a number of HM ships – frigates, minesweepers etc – in which experiments and trials were conducted. Equipment was developed for submarines and helicopters as well as surface craft.

Naval helicopters had become an integral component of the weapons systems of destroyers and frigates, and Portland was now one of the U.K.'s busiest naval ports. A Helicopter Anti-Submarine Warfare Squadron became based at Chickerell, Weymouth, in 1957. Then 737 Helicopter Squadron of Whirlwind helicopters was formed at Portland, and construction started on the nation's first naval helicopter station at the Mere, one of the D-Day embarkation points at the south-west shore of the harbour. A landing strip was formed from playing fields, two hangars were built and a large fleet canteen became the operations centre. 24 April 1959 was an auspicious day for the Royal Navy in Dorset, when Admiral Sir Manley Power, the C-in-C Portsmouth, commissioned the Royal Naval Air Station, being absorbed into HMS *Osprey*. Before the first year was out no less than nine helicopters had dropped from the sky. Pilots who survived the ditching became members of the exclusive 'Goldfish Club'.

Five days after the opening of the RN Air Station in April 1959, the Queen and Prince Charles arrived for the commissioning of Britain's largest warship, HMS *Eagle*. After the formalities the young prince steered the aircraft carrier out in the Channel. 16 years later as the Prince of Wales, HRH Prince Charles had command of his own ship at Portland, HMS *Bronington*. Among his tasks in this wooden-hulled coastal minesweeper was monitoring Soviet submarines in the Channel.

World attention focused on Portland's Admiralty Underwater Weapons Establishment in 1961, in one of the classic spy cases of all time, featuring microdots, secret maps, dead-letter boxes and documents passed to Russian agents. In an 8-day trial at the Old Bailey, it emerged that Harry Houghton of Wyke Regis and Portlander Ethel Gee were the first links in a Soviet spy network. Neither was in a high position but they had access to top secret records. They passed material about British submarines to Gordon Lonsdale, a professional Russian agent, who then sent it to the USSR by a high powered transmitter hidden in the Ruislip home of Peter and Helen Kroger. The Portland ring was allowed to continue until Gee was arrested with her shopping bag full of film and photographs, including details of the nuclear submarine, *Dreadnought*.

The case shook the whole of the NATO alliance, and led to a strict tightening of counter espionage security. Ethel Gee, 46, insisted she was no traitor but was merely infatuated with her love for Houghton. When Lord Chief Justice Parker passed sentences of 20-25 years on the ringleaders, and 15 years each on the local pair, he remarked that it '. . . had all the characteristics of a thriller.' Lonsdale and the Krogers were later exchanged for Britons held in Russia, and the lovers were married soon after their release in 1970.

Earlier, in March 1957 Prince Charles's great-uncle, the First Sea Lord, Earl Mountbatten, drove from Romsey to Portland Naval Base, a visit which was to change the course of the Royal Navy's role in Dorset. Some in the Admiralty had doubted the value of Portland as a naval base, but after watching manoeuvres and exercises aboard the air defence ship HMS *Salisbury*, Mountbatten was in no doubt. Many of Portland's assets were unmatched; its fine harbour with minimal tides; proximity to open sea; well equipped berths; facilities for fuelling, small ship repairs and recreation; degaussing and noise ranges, and half a century of anti-submarine development. Mountbatten regarded this as an ideal training base.

Traditionally sea exercises had been *ad hoc*, with crews often regarding trials as battles of wits to convince the monitors of their efficiency. A revolution in the working up of Her Majesty's ships was heralded by Lord Mountbatten's 1958 White Paper 'The Way Ahead'. A new organisation under a Flag Officer Sea Training introduced a new rigorous exercise system. For four decades the acronym 'FOST' was said to make the 'hardiest of naval souls quake in their steaming boots'. The first Flag Officer Sea Training was Vice Admiral Sir William Crawford, and in the autumn of 1958 the first ship to be subject to FOST was the Salisbury-Class aircraft detection frigate HMS *Llandaff*.

The frigate HMS Llandaff made history in 1958 as the first ship to be put through the rigours of FOST regime at Portland. The intensely realistic sea training was said to make the 'hardiest of naval souls quake in their steaming boots', setting the standard for all NATO navies.

Ships were tested at the beginning of their commission, and complex 'threats' with many unexpected and surprise war scenarios tested the initiative of officers and crews alike. Tasks often involved sailing on two or three triangular obstacle courses – intercepted by 'enemy' forces to produce some 'interesting incidents.' Day or night, ships could be subject to surprise attacks by submarines, planes and helicopters – compounded by simulated attacks by destroyers and fast patrol boats. A particularly hard task was when the ships crossed an area of 'nuclear fallout' in a closed down state while still under attack. So realistic were the challenges that nobody in a ship's company could escape surprise, shock and terror in equal measures. The work-up programme lasted up to eight weeks, but the action peaked in the weekly 'Thursday War'.

The FOST system at Portland was so successful that it set world standards in the training and work-up of ships, and over the years every NATO country sent ships there to be prepared to a high state of readiness. The exercises were extremely expensive to run, and input from foreign ships made a useful contribution to the Navy's finances. FOST set the course of Britain's seaborne naval training for the next 40 years, but the 'Way Ahead' review had its downside for the area. With a reduced Navy there was less need for repair, refit and docking facilities. Portland's last floating dock No. 26 was towed away in 1959 after 4 years at the port, having lifted more than 80 vessels of up to 2700 tons. Within two years the main part of Portland Dockyard was closed with the loss of hundreds of jobs.

TWELVE

NEW HORIZONS

The Royal Marines are respected as an elite corps specialising in amphibious warfare. They are invariably at the heart of some of the most dangerous campaigns, and are prepared for action anywhere in the world. When in 1954 they needed a new base for amphibious training they took over the old wartime base of HMS *Turtle* at Poole.

The school expanded in 1956 as the Joint Service Amphibious Warfare Centre, and in July 1973 it became *Royal Marines Poole*. A further reorganisation in 2001 created 1 *Assault Group Royal Marines*, responsible for all the Assault Squadrons on the Landing Platform Dock Ship HMS *Albion*, and in HMS *Ocean*. The 27,000 tonnes *Ocean*, the largest ship in the Royal Navy at her launch in 1995, was specifically designed to support amphibious landing operations of RM commandos, and so became extensively used by the assault marines from Poole. They specialise in the handling and navigation of craft from small, fast assault boats, up to the heavy lift landing vessels of over 100 tons, prior to deployment with the fleet.

Hamworthy, Poole, is also the home of the select and clandestine Special Boat Service (SBS). Together with other RM branches the 4-squadrons of the SBS have played a crucial part in every counter-terrorism and war action involving the Royal Navy, and their personnel often serve for a year or more in actions in dangerous hotspots such as Afghanistan. Their missions are so covert that when a senior commando was killed in 2009 even his funeral was kept secret. The SBS used the Second World War veteran HMS *Rame Head* moored in Portland Harbour for armed boarding, underwater demolitions anti-terrorist and anti-piracy exercises. Regular SBS practice continued at Portland after the closure of the Naval Base, using the Falklands veteran ex-RFA *Sir Tristram*.

A new weapon in the SBS armoury was tested at Poole in 2009; a 'terrifyingly fast' stealth boat, on course for operations in numerous theatres of war around the world. This superboat was destined to insert and extract troops, patrol dangerous waters and hunt down drug smugglers – an escalating role for the Royal Navy.

The contrast with the Navy's earlier big ships could not be greater. After the last battleship *Vanguard* left the scene, the Royal Navy's largest ever British aircraft carriers, *Eagle* (1951-1972) and *Ark Royal* (1950-1978) were regular visitors to Dorset. These last conventional fixed-wing aircraft carriers were superseded by three smaller carriers, HMS *Invincible*, HMS *Illustrious* and the new *Ark Royal*, all

Men of the Special Boat Service training in Poole Harbour near their Hamworthy base.

of which worked up to peak efficiency at Portland.

Yet another naval aviation milestone was passed off Dorset in April 1963. A Hawker Siddeley Kestrel, a revolutionary vertical takeoff and landing aircraft and prototype of the Harrier, made the first ever VTOL deck landing, on HMS *Ark Royal* sailing east of the Shambles. After the development of the Sea Harrier VTOL there were fears that this extremely noisy aircraft would be based at Portland's Royal Naval Air Station. The RN's helicopters did not create such a noise problem as their flight paths avoided the built-up areas across South Dorset. There was relief ashore when the Fleet Air Arm confirmed that the Sea Harrier would not be stationed on the island.

NATO's power was always greater than the sum of its parts, so the formation of the world's first permanent multinational naval squadron was a logical move. The inauguration ceremony for the 'Standing Naval Force Atlantic' took place in 1968 at the Portland Naval Base; an honour indeed for Dorset. In this force, ships from all the Atlantic Alliance nations trained and operated as a single team. Standing NATO Maritime Group 1 (SNMG1) as it is now called, continues in the twenty-first century as a unique model of international naval cooperation.

The RN helicopter base at Portland grew from strength to strength. In a five-year expansion 1969 to 1974 thousands of tons of stone were tipped into the edge of the harbour at the Mere, adding 12 acres of runway and landing areas. HMS *Osprey* was now the largest and busiest helicopter base in Europe, and over three decades no less than twelve training squadrons prepared both aircrews and

By the 1960s fears were mounting of surprise attacks on British ships by small but powerful hostile craft. In response the Royal Navy ordered *Scimitar*, *Sabre* and *Cutlass* in 1969 to form the First Fast Training Boat (F.T.B) Squadron, based at Portland.

ground crews for front line service in frigates and destroyers.

Russian spy ships were active in the Channel, and in November 1974 they attempted to seize a helicopter which had crashed south of Portland Bill. They were thwarted by HMS *Reclaim* which located and recovered the machine from under the Soviets' noses.

The invention of the hovercraft created universal excitement, and as early as 1959 a Saunders Roe machine was demonstrated to the Royal Navy at Portland. Eventually the BH7 Mk.2 hovercraft (37 tonnes, 80 knots) was developed as a naval minehunter, and in 1983 delegates from 10 NATO countries watched successful

The destroyer HMS *Devonshire* leaving Portland Harbour in October 1967. Behind the Westland Wessex helicopter (aft deck) is her Sea Slug guided missile system.

A formation of Wessex HAS 3 helicopters over Portland breakwater.

trials of this craft in Portland Harbour.

In 1971 a strange-looking 3,400-tonnes vessel with a block-like aft superstructure, was towed into Portland Harbour. Motionless on a fixed mooring, RDV *Crystal* was an underwater acoustic research laboratory used by AUWE/DRA scientists.

A succession of helicopter types was introduced at the RNAS for anti-submarine warfare, training and ship-to-shore personnel transport, supporting destroyers

October 1973, HMS *Achilles* passes the old Breakwater Fort as she enters Portland Harbour. The Leander class frigate was later sold to Chile.

HMS *Invincible* on trials in West Bay off Portland in February 1982. Two months later the carrier was thrust into action in the Falklands conflict. On the way she nearly fired a missile at a Brazilian airliner mistakenly identified as Argentinian. The incident was dismissed as being merely an 'inconvenience to passengers' underwear . . .'

and frigates. From 1964 robust torpedo-carrying Wasps became the mainstay; they were especially formidable when carrying guided missiles. The Westland Whirlwind was the first British helicopter built specifically for submarine detection duties and it could also carry torpedoes. Then came the more powerful Wessex Mk.3, with its advanced radar and dipping sonar devices. The Mk. 5 version was used in commando roles, and from 1976 made a huge impact on safety on the Dorset coast with its search and rescue (SAR) activities.

Westland's joint venture with the French resulted in the immensely successful Lynx, a fast all-weather multipurpose helicopter introduced to the Royal Navy at Portland in 1976.

The remote British Falkland Islands were invaded by Argentina on 2 April 1982, triggering the Falklands War. The rigorous training and exercises provided by FOST immediately proved their worth; virtually all the Royal Navy's combat ships active in the Falklands conflict had been worked up at Portland. Among the numerous ships that came to Dorset for trials and preparation were requisitioned tankers, ferries, and Royal Fleet Auxiliary ships. At the time the Navy did not have mine countermeasures (MCM) vessels capable of reaching the South Atlantic, and so five deep sea trawlers were requisitioned and fitted with minesweeping equipment. These ships were designated the 11th MCM Squadron and sailed from Portland for the Falklands on 27 April 1982.

One of the first vessels to leave the UK for the Falklands was the Admiralty's Portland-based ocean-going tug RMAS *Typhoon*. With just two days notice and manned by civilians from Portland this little ship raced to the battle zone, where she encountered storms and enormous seas. Her crew worked long and relentless hours providing vital support to the warships and the troops. One of *Typhoon*'s most poignant tasks was towing the bombed and still burning RFA *Sir Galahad* to the place where she was to be sunk as a war grave.

A few months earlier, after a spell at Portland, HMS *Sheffield* had spent time next to an Argentine crew. One officer recalled 'When we heard that we were fighting Argentina, it seemed very strange. A year ago, they were our friends; now we were fighting them.' *Sheffield* was the first RN ship lost through enemy action since 1945.

After picking up survivors from the bombed HMS *Antelope*, many with horrible injuries, one captain remarked 'throughout the whole thing it was noticeable that calmness reigned supreme. Maybe all that training at Portland had paid off in the long run.'

Royal Marines with the SBS from Poole played a heroic central role in the recapture of the distant islands from the Argentinians.

Both aircrew and ground crew from HMS *Osprey*'s helicopter squadrons operated on ships in the heat of the Falklands conflict. The doomed destroyers *Sheffield* and *Coventry*, and the frigates *Ardent* and *Antelope* all carried Lynxes from *Osprey*'s 815 Squadron. The Wasp helicopters from 829 Squadron were with several ships, including the frigate HMS *Plymouth* which was hit by bombs. The 815 and 829 Squadrons were awarded battle honours for their part in the campaign to liberate the Falkland Islands. For months civilian and naval personnel at Portland and other bases worked frenetically to prepare and support vessels for the conflict zone nearly 13,000 km (8,000 miles) away.

The Falklands episode exposed the country's fallacy of concentrating on the perceived threat from the Soviet Union in Europe while disregarding more far-flung areas of potential conflict. Good as it was, the FOST work-up regime had to be totally revamped in the light of the experience in the South Atlantic.

The demise of the Soviet Union and end of the Cold War radically changed the Royal Navy's outlook. This predictive quote appeared in the 'Naval Review' of 1989: 'It might lead to a quieter life for some but what about the international yobbo with his grenade launcher filled with some chemical nasty or the innocent little obscurely registered internationally-crewed freighter that uncovers its hold as it proceeds up channel and poops 10 second-hand Exocets at Thursday Divisions at Portland to further the cause of some 'Holy' War?'

The Gulf War of 1990-91 was not exactly holy, but Saddam Hussein's invasion of Kuwait called for a big naval and military response. The former Captain of HMS *Osprey*, Chris Craig in HMS *London,* led the British naval contingent of 11 destroyers, 2 submarines, 10 mine-countermeasure vessels, 3 patrol craft, 11 Royal fleet auxiliaries and 3 naval air squadrons. The Type 42 destroyers HM ships *Gloucester* and *Cardiff* and Type 22 frigate HMS *Brazen* were pre-eminent. Their helicopters helped destroy the bulk of the Iraqi Navy. This was one of the Royal Navy's biggest operations of the 1990s.

THIRTEEN

SAILING ON

By the late 1980s some 90 warships and auxiliaries were passing through Portland's FOST each year for exercise. There were three categories; Safety Operational Sea Training (SOST) put the ship's company through safety drills and manoeuvres; Basic Operational Sea Training (BOST) – seven weeks of intensive training exercises, stretching ships and men to the limit, and Continuation Operational Sea Training (COST), an annual refresher course for operational ships.

Generations of kings and royal princes gained their naval experiences in Dorset.

Prince Andrew followed his elder brother Prince Charles by joining the Royal Navy in 1979. After active service as a helicopter pilot in the Falklands War, he transferred to the Lynx at the Portland Naval Air Station in 1983. Four years later he became Helicopter Warfare Instructor of 702 Naval Air Squadron at *Osprey*. In 1990 now as the Duke of York, he was appointed flight commander/pilot of the Lynx on HMS *Campbeltown*, the flagship of the North Atlantic NATO force. The Lynx of 815 and 829 Squadrons of the RNAS Portland operated as ships' flights, including on the new Type 23 frigates. The air station now employed 1500 personnel and was also home to 772 Squadron with its Sea King Mk 4 helicopters. These were used for transporting personnel and stores for FOST, as well as flight deck and sea acceptance trials, photography and search and rescue.

For deck landing practice a floating platform, *Aircraft Lighter* 50, nicknamed *Duck*, was moored near the helicopter base. In February 1984 to celebrate 50,000 deck landings, the Commanding Officer of *Osprey*, Captain Tony Wigley, made a ceremonial landing in a Lynx helicopter. Considering the frenzied nature of sea training, accidents were remarkably rare. Dorset's naval and civilian population were therefore shocked to learn that the popular Captain Wigley was killed when his helicopter crashed into Portland Breakwater on 3 December 1984.

Having given a firm assurance in March 1982 that there were no plans to run down or close Portland Naval Base, the Navy embarked on a major development scheme, including a new HQ for the Queen's Harbourmaster and £30m accommodation buildings for officers and ratings at Castletown.

No sooner had the new works at Portland been completed in 1989 than the Cold War ended, causing a rapid reappraisal of Western forces. The Royal Navy had declined in strength steadily since 1960 when it was still the world's second-largest Navy. Now in 1990 the government used the 'Peace Dividend' opportunity to force through unprecedented cuts in defence expenditure. The plan was to

An aerial view of Portland Naval Base, with ships dressed overall for a Navy Day. Queens Pier (nearest) was completed within seven years of the end of the Second World War. Beyond are the old Coaling Pier and the jetties constructed at various phases. The port was always constrained by the lack of flat land, partly redressed by reclamation (right).

reduce Royal Navy/Royal Marines to some 60,000 personnel, a reduction of 18%. In fact, from 1992 the Navy lost 33% of its uniformed personnel, down to 41,000 in 1997. Over the same period the frigate/destroyer force reduced from 45 to 35 ships; three of our 15 nuclear submarines were taken out of service, and the conventional submarine force was completely eliminated.

A highlight of the year for thousands of Dorset people was the annual Portland Navy Days. At their peak tens of thousands of people attended the two-day events, and the last Navy Days in July 1990 was still a spectacular occasion. Air displays included the Battle of Britain and the Royal Naval Historical Flights. A Vulcan bomber flew low over the crowds; a deafening Harrier jump jet hovered improbably over the harbour; a Catalina flying boat landed and took off; RM commandos from Poole made realistic assaults, and spirits were lifted by the Royal Marines Band. The Navy Days were always memorable, and their demise left a gap in the county's popular tourist calendar.

The closure of Portland Naval Base was formally announced to the House of Commons on 12 November 1992. All the main naval functions, except the Marines and SBS at Poole, were to transfer from Dorset to Plymouth, although the Royal Naval Air Station, HMS *Osprey* would remain open for now.

There was vehement opposition to the closure of the Portland base, not only from the South Dorset communities who faced huge economic and job losses, but also from all ranks of naval personnel. For more than two centuries, the sea off the Dorset coast had proved ideal for the exercise of HM ships. Portland had an

The multi-million pound infrastructure of the RNAS Portland, seen here in in 1988, ensured the smooth operation of the busiest helicopter base in Europe. Two decades on, the old oil tanks and landing areas have gone, replaced by a huge maritime business park. A runway has been retained for the Coastguard Search and Rescue helicopter.

unmatched harbour of refuge and was firmly established as one of the country's prime naval ports. Its FOST training was considered the best in the world.

However the rapid changes in technology and in the nature of the sea warfare pointed to some advantages in moving the naval operations to Plymouth. In particular submarines could now be detected at a range of 200 miles, whereas the Channel off Dorset at its narrowest is only 57 miles (93 km) wide, limiting its training value. Coordination of submarine, ship and aircraft movements was considered to be easier from Plymouth with its wide arc across the Western Approaches.

NATO warships continued to exercise out of Portland to the last. The first Spanish ship to come to Portland for sea training was the *Cazadora*, which arrived in June 1993 with Spain's Chief of Naval Staff. Relationships were somewhat better than they were 405 years earlier when the Royal Navy fought off the Spanish Armada in this same area! Also on that typical exercise were the Type 23 frigate HMS *Sheffield* (originally *Bruiser*) and the Type 42 destroyers *Nottingham* and *Newcastle*, which all had to make lightning responses to fast 'attacks' by two Hunter aircraft. A vital component was the RFA tanker *Olna* which accompanied the ships.

The cuts were not confined to the uniformed Navy. In September 1992 the Admiralty confirmed that three Dorset research bases were to close; the Defence Research Agency establishments at Southwell and East Weares on Portland, and Holton Heath. The RTV *Crystal* floating laboratory had already been axed that year, but the torpedo testing facility at Bincleaves, Weymouth was to stay for the time being. Between them these facilities employed thousands of people and as with the departure of the Navy their closure would have a profound effect on the local economy.

For a century these top-secret establishments and their predecessors had played a key role in the defence of the nation, and among the post-war achievements by their scientists were underwater detection in all its forms; projects on nuclear submarines; the Sting Ray torpedo; and the anti-submarine wire-guided experimental vehicle *TVX*.

The Royal Navy finally weighed anchor at Portland Naval Base on 20 July, 1995. In beautiful sunshine the shore-side White Ensign was lowered, while a 13 gun salute echoed around the Island's East Cliffs as the last Flag Officer Sea Training, Rear Admiral John Tolhurst, sailed out of the harbour, heading for Plymouth on HMS *Argyll*.

The emotional occasion was witnessed by 11 Admirals of the Fleet, many local

Eleven Admirals of the Fleet joined the thousands who witnessed the final departure of Portland's last Flag officer Sea Training, Rear-Admiral John Tolhurst on HMS Argyll on 25 July 1995. A 13-gun salute was fired from East Weares, as he heads for Plymouth. For 36 years Dorset had honed countless ships of the Royal Navy, NATO and other navies up to supreme standards of efficiency and safety. Portland Naval base was no more.

The white ensign flies over HMS *Osprey*'s Victoria Gate entrance. The area has now been totally demilitarised and transformed into 'Osprey Quay', with the Weymouth & Portland National Sailing Academy, 600-berth Portland Marina and the Royal Yachting Association's HQ.

dignitaries and hundreds of civilian staff who were facing redundancy.

It is ironic that the savings made by the Navy's move from Dorset to Devonport made possible investment in new state-of-the-art Type 23 frigates, including one to be named HMS *Portland*. Commissioned in 2000, *Portland* rapidly developed a great affinity with Weymouth and Portland through her frequent operational and social visits. The ship's company marked their award of the Freedom of the Borough with a celebratory parade through Weymouth in 2009, and now, in 2011, Lieutenant Commander Sarah West became its commander – the first woman to be given command of a frontline frigate.

There was initial confusion over the future of the Royal Naval Air Station after assurances that it would stay. Then in July 1995 a statement by Malcolm Rifkind, Secretary of State for Defence, sealed its fate. His 'Frontline First' report announced that Portland's long association with the Royal Navy was to end. Rifkind said 'We took the decision because we found that the aircraft that were to remain at Portland could easily be accommodated at Yeovilton, together with more than two thirds of the service personnel involved. This would save around £12 million a year, with no loss of operational capability.'

Duck, the RNAS floating deck, was removed in August 1995 having taken 92,000 landings by 15 types of helicopter since 1972. That same month saw the departure of the RN Provost (naval police), and the closure of Aggie Weston's at Castletown. The 'keys' of the former Portland Naval Base were handed to the new private owner, Portland Port Ltd., on 29 March 1996.

Prince Andrew, Duke of York, returned to Dorset in 1995 as Senior Pilot of 815 Naval Air Squadron. He now commanded over 80 aircrew, 420 ground staff and 41 helicopters – the largest flying unit in the Fleet Air Arm. However the departure from Portland of naval ships left the RNAS helicopter base in some difficulty. The ships they now served and exercised with were now based 60 miles away.

In 1998 forty years of aviation at the Royal Naval Air Station, Portland, was coming to an end. To celebrate its achievements and its rapport with the Dorset community, HMS *Osprey* threw everything open for the public on 17 October. Sunshine and a fresh breeze welcomed thousands of people on the day they called the 'End of an Era' to see on display every type of helicopter which had flown there, from the earliest Westland Dragonfly to the latest Lynx. Prince Andrew landed in the maroon Sikorsky helicopter of the Queen's Flight at 1200 hours, and proceeded to inspect the displays and mingle with people. He was accompanied by *Osprey*'s final Commanding Officer, Captain John Harvey (by happy coincidence the namesake of the man who 200 years earlier had first proposed a breakwater for Portland).

A Sea Harrier showed its aerial talents and pilots of 815 Squadron gave an impressive aerobatic display. The Band of the Royal Marines Beat the Retreat, before Prince Andrew stepped up on the dais to take the final salute while the Ensign was lowered.

The run-down of HMS *Osprey* was completed on 31 Mar 1999. The CO, Captain Harvey said 'The Fleet Air Arm goes out with its head held high' before being towed off to his personal retirement on a gun carriage decorated with a sail and a rudder. A bugler sounded 'Sunset', and the Royal Navy was finally gone from Portland.

The last Lynx flew off to the west; the RN School of Helicopter Control moved to HMS *Heron*, at Yeovilton, Somerset, and the Fleet Target Group moved to HMS *Seahawk* at Culdrose, Cornwall.

Britain's largest naval air station then metamorphosed into Osprey Quay, a huge maritime business and leisure venue. Here now is the HQ of the Royal Yachting Association; a 600-berth marina; Sunseeker luxury yacht maker, and the Weymouth & Portland National Sailing Academy, the base for the 2012 Olympic Sailing events. Portland Harbour in its commercial guise is more peaceful than it has ever been, but the Royal Navy retains a few rights. Warships still visit and exercise in the area, the acoustic and degaussing ranges are still operational. The port has 'authorised' berthing for nuclear submarines, and the Royal Marines and SBS continue to do their vital training in the area from their very active Poole base.

In 2004, fourteen years after the Royal Navy put the sexes on an even keel, Dorset-born Captain Charlotte Atkinson became the first woman to command an operational UK warship. Appropriately, 32-year-old 'Charlie' was born on Trafalgar Day. She was the only woman among the 45-strong crew of HMS *Brecon* of the Third Mine Countermeasures Squadron.

The changes have been phenomenal, and in 2011 the Senior Service was facing decimation through cuts on an unprecedented scale. However, in the twenty-first century Dorset can look back with pride over the role the county has played over hundreds of years in the Royal Navy's defence of this great maritime nation.

FURTHER READING

Attwooll, Maureen and Harrison, Denise, *Weymouth and Portland at War*, Dovecote Press

Beresford, Lord Charles, *The Betrayal*, Google ebook

Broadley, A.M. and Bartelot, R.G., *Three Dorset Captains at Trafalgar*, Dovecote Press

Carter, Geoffrey, *The Royal Navy at Portland since 1845*, Maritime Books;
    The Royal Navy at Portland 1900-2000, Maritime Books

Clammer, Richard, *Cosens of Weymouth*, Vols. 1 & 2, Black Dwarf Pubications

Dyer, Bernard and Darvill, Timothy (eds*), The Book of Poole Harbour*, Dovecote Press

Franklin, George D., *Britain's Anti-submarine capability, 1919-1939*

Hill, J.R. and Ranft, Bryan, *The Oxford illustrated history of the Royal Navy*

Jackson, B.L, *The Island of Portland Railways*, Vol.1, The Oakwood Press

Marriott, Leo, *Battleships*, Igloo Books

Morris, Stuart, *Portland, An Illustrated History*, Dovecote Press
    Portland, Then & Now, Dovecote Press

Preston, Anthony, *Submarine Warfare*, Brown Books

Stevens, W.O. and Westcott, Allan, *A History of Sea Power*, Gutenberg ebook

Terraine, John, *The Life & Times of Lord Mountbatten*, Arrow Books

The Naval Review, quarterly.

ACKNOWLEDGEMENTS

I am grateful to the following for helpful advice: John Culley; David McCaughey; David MacLeod; John Cranny; Rupert Best; Arthur Copus; and especially David Burnett of The Dovecote Press.

Most of the illustrations have come from either the author's collection or The Dovecote Press collection, but I am grateful to the following for allowing the inclusion of illustrations in their possession or for which they hold the copyright: HMS *Osprey*; Royal Navy (ex-Portland); The Imperial War Museum, CT 295 (the front cover), A 24047; and The National Maritime Museum for the plan showing the Spanish Armada off Portland, F 8044.